starting with me

Topic ideas for the teaching of history, geography and religious education to children from five to seven

Barbara Hume and Annie Sevier

Illustrations by Heather Hacking

First published in 1991 by
BELAIR PUBLICATIONS LIMITED
P.O. Box, 12, Twickenham, England, TW1 2QL

© Barbara Hume and Annie Sevier

Series Editor Robyn Gordon
Designed by Richard Souper
Photography by Kelvin Freeman

Typesetting by Florencetype Ltd, Kewstoke, Avon
Printed and Bound by Heanor Gate Printing Limited

ISBN 0 947882 18 9

Acknowledgements

The authors and publishers would like to thank the children, parents and staff at Cranford Infant School, Hounslow, and East Sheen Primary School, East Sheen, Richmond-upon-Thames, for their support during the preparation of this book.

They would also like to thank Lynn Aspinall and her class at Monkscroft Infants School, Cheltenham, Gloucestershire.

Special thanks are due to Sue Rayner, Tehmina Sheikh, Tauheed Khawaja, Melanie Maclaine, Caroline Lewis and John Logan (Advisory Teacher for R.E. for the London Borough of Hounslow) for contributions and advice.

They would also like to give thanks for cover artwork to Meryl Gray, James and Lucy Allen and Lauren Fogarty.

The authors and publishers wish to thank the following for permission to use copyright material.

Curtis Brown Ltd. on behalf of the author for 'Mango' from *Come Into My Tropical Garden* by Grace Nichols, A & C Black. © 1988 Grace Nichols;

Spike Milligan Productions Ltd, for 'Bump' by Spike Milligan;

Scholastic Publications Ltd. for 'Father says . . .' from *Mind Your Own Business* by Michael Rosen, Andre Deutsch Ltd.;

Ian Serraillier for 'First Foot' from *Let's Celebrate* ed. John Foster, OUP;

Walker Books Ltd. for 'The Grass House' from *Out and About* by Shirley Hughes. © 1988 Shirley Hughes.

Peter Young for 'Hands' in *Passwords*, Oliver and Boyd, 1974.

Contents

Introduction

Starting with Me presents teachers with ideas for helping children to understand the world in which they live. The topics covered explore different times and places. They also aim to give value to the children as individuals, and to encourage them to respect others of different races, religions and cultures.

The book is divided into four sections: the first section covers topics that are central to each individual child; the second section focuses on the child's immediate social contacts – family and friends; the third section builds on the children's wider experiences of the world; and the final section takes a look at community festivals.

Most of the topics in this book centre on the Humanities, but all have built-in links with other curriculum areas.

All the topics rely on teachers 'exploiting' to the full the resources that they have to hand – mainly the children, their families and the local community – while always being ready to extend the children's experiences by introducing them to new ideas, perhaps through a penfriend project, or by celebrating a festival hitherto unexplored.

Many of the ideas contained within the topics interlink. For example, a topic on journeys could be timed to culminate with either the Christmas journey to Bethlehem or the celebration of Passover. The topic on Hands and the idea of 'helping hands' could be related to the Muslim concern for helping the poor and the celebration of Eid-ul-Fitr.

Some of the chapters contain stories which can be dramatised and the accompanying activities and display work could form the basis for assemblies.

Barbara Hume and Annie Sevier
1991

Myself

Discussion/Starting points

Read *But Martin* by June Counsel, Picture Corgi, and *Elmer* by David McKee, Arrow Books. Talk about similarities and differences between individuals. How would you describe yourself to a new friend? (or penfriend). What kind of things would you describe? e.g. appearance, interests, hobbies, family details etc. Talk about the uniqueness of individuals. Introduce the topic of personal history by reading stories and poems about babies and young children such as *I Want my Potty* and *Oscar got the Blame* by Tony Ross, Andersen Press, and the poems of Michael Rosen. Share memories of early childhood, discussing similarities and differences. Talk about the essential needs of all human beings to sustain health and happiness. Talk about thoughts, opinions, likes and dislikes, feelings, and our need to express ourselves.

Vocabulary

Humanity, people, human race, fellow, individual, person, character, personality, male, female, features, appearance, expression, complexion, behaviour, profile, silhouette, image, identity, make-up, unique, originality, eccentricity, trait, private, personal, self, ego, yours truly, opinion, point of view, imagination, mind.

Collections

Photographs, favourite toys, favourite story books, family albums, mementoes, souvenirs, baby clothes, hospital identity bracelets, old birthday cards, cake decorations (e.g. wedding, christening, birthday), first shoes etc.

Activities

- Self portraits.
  - Paint self-portraits (head and shoulders) using water colours. Mix paints to make different skin tones, eye and hair colours. Design a frame or mount for the self portrait.
  - Paint full-size pictures. Display at child height around the classroom or along corridors. Draw speech bubbles coming from each child. Children dictate or write text introducing themselves to the rest of the school.

- Take photographs of each child at the beginning of term. Mount photographs in a class album with a written commentary describing each child.

● Make personal time-lines to show date of birth and important events e.g. starting nursery, birth of siblings, starting school, holidays etc. Collect photographs, postcards and mementoes and match them to the time-line.

● Write a personal diary or journal. Describe an event from your own personal point of view, an eye-witness account e.g. of an outing, the summer fair, a sports day or celebration. Compare your account with that of your friend, or with an adult. Draw pictures and mount on eye-shaped paper as shown in photograph on previous page.

● Read extracts from *I Like this Poem*, ed. by Kaye Webb, Puffin. Write a personal response to a poem, story or a painting. Collect responses into a class anthology.

● Collect data about the favourite things of your classmates and make graphs e.g. favourite sports, authors, television programmes, fruits, breakfast cereals, toys etc.

● Read story *But Martin* by June Counsel. Write your own story about a visiting alien, substituting the names of your friends and emphasising the differences between individuals.

● Read the story *Elmer* by David McKee. Design a patterned elephant. Make sure that your elephant is unique. Display the different elephants together.

● Measure parts of the body. Make graphs and charts. Measure how far you can reach, jump or throw things. Count how many things you can pick up with each hand.

THE FIVE SENSES

Arrange a multi-sensory week of experiences. Allocate a day to each of the five senses and prepare a range of activities associated with that sense. Alternatively, the class can be divided into five groups and rotated throughout the week.

- Smell: play a 'guess the fruit' game. Record on worksheet by putting the number of the yoghurt pot on the fruit shape.

- Sight: Make 'disco spectacles'. Design and make some glasses. Use different coloured Cellophane to look through and change the colour of your world. Write a story about your 'magic glasses'.

- Sound: Play a listening game or go on a 'listening walk' – draw a map of your journey and write down or draw the noises you hear.

- Taste: See chapter on Passover.

- Touch: See chapter on Hands.

Art and Craft

● Make silhouettes of profiles using an overhead projector.

● Whole body shadow portraits. Draw around your shadow and paint.

● Print using hands, fingers, feet.

● Plaster cast hand prints.

● Make puppets.

● Skeleton pictures: printing white on black paper.

● Design a favourite outfit – for taking part in a favourite sport or pastime.

Names

Can you find our names hidden in our paintings?

Discussion/Starting points

Why are our names special to us? Why do we need names? Talk about different kinds of names and introduce vocabulary such as surname, first, second and middle names, 'Christian' name, family name, maiden name, Mr, Mrs, Miss, Ms, title, signature, initials. Investigate naming ceremonies in different religions. Ask children to find out how their first names were decided upon. Is it a common name in the family? Research famous namesakes and the meanings (origins) of first names – a name dictionary is useful here. Look at your family name – does it have any specific meaning that you can discover? (Many surnames originate from place-names or occupations). Where do you find lists of names? When do we need to write our names as signatures? Talk about nicknames. This is a good opportunity to talk about showing sensitivity and not hurting people's feelings. Read the story *A Porcupine named Fluffy* by Helen Lester, Picturemac. Discuss the naming of pets. Talk about capital letters – used for proper nouns.

Activities

A	Georgia	Milap	U
Billy	Guy	Nafeesa	Vincent
C	H	O	W
Daniel	I	Persephone	X
Duncan	James	Q	Yumi
Edine	Jodie		
Elliott	Julia	Richard	Z
Emma	Kim	S	
F	L	Tali	

- Arrange first names in alphabetical order. The easiest way to do this with young children is to go through the alphabet listing names to make a chart as shown.

- How many children have names beginning with E?
  Make a simple bar chart using name cards written by the children.

- Make a graph. How many letters are there in your first name? Use squared paper for recording.

			Edine
		David	Elliot
	Billy	Duncan	Emma

A   B   C   D   E

D	u	n	c	a	n					
P	e	r	s	e	p	h	o	n	e	
Y	u	m	i							
1	2	3	4	5	6	7	8	9	10	11

Number of letters

Names

- Look for names in the environment. Look for the maker's name on objects, signatures on paintings, name plaques on buildings, shop names, brand names, names of houses and boats, the names on gravestones, foundation stones and memorials. Can you find any streets, buildings or schools in your locality that are named after famous people? Investigate their history.
- Make a name tree. Record the names of your family (grandparents, parents, siblings) as far back as you can go. Design a tree shape round your chart.

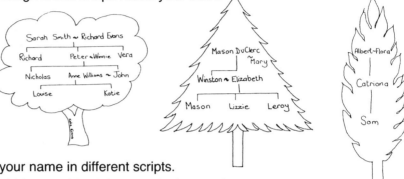

- Find out how to write your name in different scripts.
- Make a word search – hide your friends' names in the puzzle.

V	B	A	R	B	A	R	A	U
I	C	B	O	T	N	L	U	T
S	V	C	B	D	N	E	E	S
F	G	A	Y	H	I	I	J	X
K	L	H	N	O	E	P	Q	R

- Clap rhythms of your names. Play a guessing game.
- Make a symmetrical print of your name. Paint your name using thick, black paint mixed with PVA glue. Fold in half and press to print – do this for each letter while the paint is still wet.
  Colour in the spaces with paint to creat a symmetrical pattern (see photograph on previous page).
- Design a bookplate, a place-card or drawer label with your name on it.
- Make 'name mobiles' using the cut out letters of your name.
- Make jumbled name pictures. Cut out the letters of your name using different kinds of paper, card, foils, felt and materials. Arrange the letters to make a picture-puzzle.
- Young children
  - write names in the sand
  - write names in paint on the table and take a print from it
  - write name/initials with a glue pen and sprinkle with glitter, sand, sawdust.
- Have fun with your initials!
  - Make the letter shapes with multilink cubes (any construction toys)
  - make your initials into a picture
  - make a printing block (potato cut-out, card or string block)
  - find out which capital letters are symmetrical
  - embroider a book mark with your initials
  - make a badge
  - make your initials with dough. Bake, paint and varnish
  - make and decorate a tile. Press shape of initials into the clay using beads etc.
  - pasta picture. Make your initials with the pasta shapes and spray with gold/silver paint.

Feelings

Musical instruments to accompany shadow puppet play. Cheese box tambourines, painted coconut shells, bell and broom handle shakers, terracotta plantpot 'bells' and drink can shakers.

Discussion/Starting points

Talk about how the children are feeling today. Encourage them to recall how they felt on their first day at school, how they feel on Christmas Eve or the night before their birthday.

Talk about 'good' and 'bad' feelings. Sometimes we have 'mixed' feelings. Ask children if they can recall specific instances. List feelings as they are mentioned, e.g. sad, bored, embarrassed, jealous, angry, impatient, disappointed, excited, interested, happy, delighted, grateful, relieved.

What makes you feel happy, sad or excited? How do you show your feelings? Talk about facial expressions, body postures, actions, e.g. sulking, smiling, laughing, nodding, winking, hugging, kissing, holding hands. How do people express their feelings? e.g. by writing letters, poetry and diaries, by sending cards and by doing things for others. Have your feelings ever been hurt? What can you do to make yourself feel better? Sometimes children will take the opportunity to express feelings of grief, sadness and loss.

How do animals show their feelings? Talk about children's pets and the signals they give.

Activities

- Collect and list as many words as you can to describe laughing and crying, e.g. giggle, hoot, chuckle, chortle, cackle, split one's sides, shrieks of laughter; wail, weep, sob, floods of tears, bawl.

- Look in a mirror. Observe closely how your face changes as you make different expressions, e.g. happy, sad, excited, surprised, angry, puzzled, frightened. Look at your mouth, eyebrows and forehead and draw what you see.

- Collect pictures showing expressive faces. Cut them in half horizontally. Can you tell how people are feeling just by looking at their eyes, or just by looking at their mouths? Play a guessing game. Cover your mouth with a piece of card and make different expressions while your partner plays at being a detective.

- Make masks. Study masks from different cultures and look how the expression is achieved.

- Write a joke book full of funny stories that would make people laugh.

- Read a story or a poem such as 'The Watch' by Michael Rosen, from *Quick, let's get out of here*, Puffin, and list all the feelings the hero experiences e.g. excitement, horror, fear, resentment, anger, guilt and shame.

- Write a 'feelings' diary for a day and illustrate it.

ANGER

Discussion/Starting points

Read *Angry Arthur* by Hiawyn Oram, Puffin, and *The Magic Finger* by Roald Dahl, Puffin.

What makes you 'see red'? What would you change if you had the power of the magic finger? Read the description of baby Eddie's 'wobbly' or tantrum in 'Eddie and the Birthday' a poem by Michael Rosen from *Quick, let's get out of here*. Why do two-year-olds often have tantrums? Collect as many 'angry' words as you can e.g. furious, cross, sullen, wild, sulky, mad, grumbling, annoyed, vexed, livid, fuming, nettled, ratty, shirty, fly off the handle, let off steam, hopping mad, hot under the collar, in a stew, tizzy or paddy. Note how many refer to heat images e.g. 'in a boiling rage'. Look at the imagery used in *Angry Arthur* of storms, typhoons and hurricanes.

Is anger a good or bad feeling? Talk about whether anger can be used in a positive way (to protest against a wrong, as a defence mechanism, to protect, or as a release of emotion).

What do you notice about your body when you are angry? Talk about the need to control your emotions. Can you stop yourself getting angry? – counting to ten, etc.

Can you remember a time when someone was angry with you? How did you feel? What did they say? Read 'Father Says' by Michael Rosen, from *A First Poetry Book*, OUP. Do animals show anger? Talk about the facial expressions of anger such as gnashing teeth, glaring, frowning, scowling and glowering together with the sounds of anger such as growling, snarling, shouting, roaring, barking and snapping.

Activities

- Collect phrases people use when they are angry, and display sayings in speech bubbles along with portraits (see photograph).

> **Father says**
>
> Father says
> Never
> Let
> me
> see
> you
> doing
> that
> again
> father says
> tell you once
> tell you a thousand times
> come hell or high water
> his finger drills my shoulder
> never let me see you doing that again.
>
> My brother knows all his little sayings off by heart
> so we practise them in bed at night.
>
> Michael Rosen

- Read 'Father Says' by Michael Rosen and talk about the way the poem is set out on the page to help us know how the angry words were spoken. Write an angry poem and try and make your poem look like it sounds using devices such as lettering that becomes larger, and words written at angles (to denote 'hopping mad').

- Write an *Angry Arthur* story in cartoon form.
- Write 'If I had the power of the Magic Finger I would . . .' on shaped paper. Mount on bright red paper.

- Write angry letters of complaint e.g. concerning an environmental or conservation issue.
- Paint 'seeing red' pictures, splatter painting in reds , yellows, and oranges.
- Make collages from cut-out-pictures – so that they look like 'exploding' pictures – such as those in *Angry Arthur*.

Feelings

- Make angry music with percussion instruments.
- Music and Movement: make up an 'angry' dance.
- Make paper bag masks of fierce, angry faces.

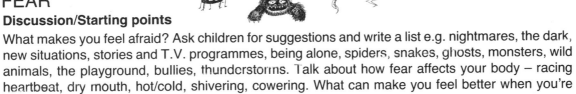

FEAR

Discussion/Starting points

What makes you feel afraid? Ask children for suggestions and write a list e.g. nightmares, the dark, new situations, stories and T.V. programmes, being alone, spiders, snakes, ghosts, monsters, wild animals, the playground, bullies, thunderstorms. Talk about how fear affects your body – racing heartbeat, dry mouth, hot/cold, shivering, cowering. What can make you feel better when you're afraid? Do animals show fear? Look at how different species protect themselves from danger. Collect words that describe fear, e.g. scared, horrified, nervous, butterflies, willies, collywobbles, creeps, heebie-jeebies, knees-knocking, petrified, white as a sheet, hair standing on end, terrified, shaking like a leaf/jelly; quaking in one's shoes; with one's heart in one's mouth etc. Talk about the imagery of coldness e.g. in a cold sweat, frozen, feel one's blood run cold, get cold feet.

Activities

- Read 'Bump' by Spike Milligan in *A Very First Poetry Book*, OUP.

> **Bump**
>
> Things that go 'bump' in the night,
> Should not really give one a fright.
> It's the hole in each ear
> That lets in the fear,
> That, and the absence of light!
>
> Spike Milligan

- Talk about the kind of noises that might frighten us (wind, music, footsteps). Read *The Owl who was afraid of the Dark* by J. Tomlinson, Methuen/Young Puffin. Talk about how the owl overcame his fears and the positive aspects of night and the dark.

Feelings

- Make 'spooky' music with percussion instruments. Make a tape with sound effects, that might accompany a ghost story.
- Make a lift-the-flap book. Write a spooky story and lift the flaps to reveal the characters.
- Write accounts of nightmares and frightening dreams.
- Make monster masks (ghosts, skeletons, monsters, dragons).
- Make shadow monsters. Draw around shadows of children making monster shapes (either individually or in groups). Paint the silhouettes, cut and display.
- With older children, look at devices used in stories and films to build up suspense and menace, e.g. music, sound effects, 'cliffhanger' endings to chapters.
- Read the story *Bears in the Night* by S. & J. Berenstain, Collins.
  - Make a shadow puppet theatre and use it to act out the story. (See page 72 for instructions.)
  - Draw a map of the bears' journey or make a 3D model.

Hands

Discussion/Starting points

Read the poem 'Hands' by Peter Young in *A First Poetry Book*, OUP.

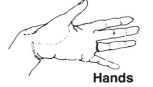

Hands

Hands
handling
dangling in water
making and shaking
slapping and clapping
warming and warning
hitting and fitting
grabbing and rubbing
peeling and feeling
taking and breaking
helping and giving
lifting
sifting sand
hand holding
hand.

Peter Young

Children act out the poem as it is read. Discuss the actions and how the children interpreted the words. Can you suggest any more pairs of words that the poet could have used? What can we do with our hands? What is special about the human hand? Look at your hands. Name the different parts: fingers, thumb, palm, wrist, knuckles, skin, nails, cuticles, fist, index finger etc. Count the number of joints on each digit. Look at how your skin moves as you flex your hand. Are all your fingernails the same shape? Look carefully at your fingertips through a hand lens. Hold your partner's hand at the end of the poem. What does it feel like? Compare your hand with an adult's hand. What differences can you see?

Vocabulary

Research the meaning of 'hand' sayings: 'hand to mouth', 'hand over fist', 'hand that rocks the cradle', 'hand in glove', 'rule of thumb', 'thumbs up/down', 'finger in every pie', 'the finger of suspicion', 'handful', 'hand-me-down'. Digit, ambidextrous, dexterity, manufacture (original meaning), manual, manuscript.

Collections

- Different kinds of glove or hand protectors, e.g. oven gloves, rubber gloves, woollen gloves and mittens, ski mittens, muffs, surgical gloves, motor cyclist's gauntlets, thimbles (including money-counting rubber thimble), hand creams, finger bandages.
- Different kinds of tools, together with hand-made items.

Activities

- Make a chart to show the different parts of the hand. Draw round your hand and label.
- What can we do with our hands? Make a chart or word bank for action words. Write each word on a cut-out hand shape. Mount back to back and hang on strings, or use to border a display.
- 'Helping hands' display. Talk about all the things we can do with our hands to help others at home and at school. Display writing and illustrations on large hand-shaped pieces of paper. Mount on backing papers that have been stencilled with hand shapes (sponge over cut-out hand shapes).
- Take your own fingerprints (by pressing lightly on an inked pad). Compare the patterns made by each of your fingers. Compare your prints with those of your friend.

Hands

- Talk about 'handedness'. Sort children according to their dominant hand. Research the handedness of family members to see if any patterns emerge. Talk about ambidexterity. Investigate dominant feet and eyes (e.g. which foot do you use to kick or dribble a ball? Which eye do you use to look through a tube?) Compare the performance of each of your hands carrying out simple tasks, e.g. putting pegs into a pegboard in one minute, or picking up handfuls of cubes. Record results by sticking gummed shapes onto handshapes as shown in the line drawing. Compare your dominant hand with non-dominant hand.

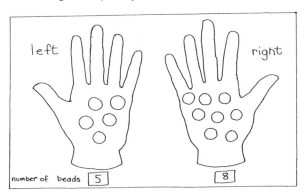

- Compare hand sizes within the family. Draw round hands of each family member. Measure length of hand, or length of hand span. Make a book, *My family of hands* (include grandparents, uncles, aunts, friends and neighbours). Ask children to bring in their mittens that they wore when they were babies. Display their present-day gloves or hand shapes to show 'Look how I've changed!'

- Investigate other ways of measuring hands. Measure the length of each finger. Measure how high the water rises in a jug when you put your hand into it up to the wrist. Draw round your hand on squared paper and count the number of squares covered by your hand.

- Investigate gloves. How can hands be protected? Make a collection of gloves and finger protectors. Investigate the different materials used for different purposes. Devise, with care, a test for insulation properties. Test the effectiveness of the materials as insulators. Look at the thickness of ski-mittens and oven gloves. Talk about the 'hardness' of thimbles, 'toughness' of motor cycle gloves, the 'flexibility' of surgical gloves, the rough texture of a money-teller's thimble etc. Look at how different hand protectors are shaped and designed to suit different purposes. Try and carry out tasks wearing different kinds of gloves and hand protectors.

- Design and make a pair of mittens to fit your hands. How can you make them fit? Print with different (old) gloves. Ask your friends to guess which glove you printed with.

- Touch and texture. Collect descriptive words e.g. hot, cold, warm, rough, smooth, sticky, bumpy, prickly, wet, dry, damp, clammy, velvety, knobbly, sharp, bendy, hard, soft. Set up a 'feely' table. Organise the opportunity for children to feel objects inside a bag or box and describe and identify them. Record observations and display in speech bubbles around the activity table. Objects to be felt might include solid shapes, jelly, treacle or honey, water, ice cubes; different fabrics, e.g. lace, knitted fabrics, fur-fabric, velvet, nylon, elastic; different types of paper, coins; materials, e.g. wood, plastic, rubber, leather; fruits and vegetables; sandpaper letters of the alphabet.

- Investigate: Which part of your hand is best for touching?

- Take rubbings of different surfaces at home and at school. Make individual books of rubbings, or use them to mount written work around the activity table.

- Make individual collages using fabrics and textured papers, pasta shapes, shells, sand and glitter etc. Display together to make a 'texture wall' to be explored (carefully) by everyone.

- Investigate the Braille alphabet. Borrow books from the library for a short time. Borrow a Braille typewriter.

- Tell the story of *The Blind Men and the Elephant*, an Indian folk tale.

Hands

The Story of the Mendhi Bush.

- Tell the story of the Mendhi bush. Make a wall story with decorative borders as shown in the photograph. Decorate hands using the mixture described on page 53. Make a display of decorated hand-shapes – use orange and brown inks or felt-tipped pens to make patterns on hand-shaped paper.
- Talk about festivals and celebrations when hands are decorated.
- Talk about the significance of rings and bracelets in many different religious ceremonies and customs, e.g. christening bracelets, wedding rings, engagement and eternity rings, Sikh Karas and rakhri bracelets.
- Make a collection of rings, bracelets and bangles.
- Design and make bracelets e.g.
  - dye pasta and thread on to elastic
  - make cylindrical clay beads. Make a hole for threading
  - thread screwed up tissue paper and pieces of foil.
- Use your hands and fingers to print with.
- Make thumb pots with clay.
- Investigate hand signals and signs, the use of hands in mime, dance, gesture and sign language.
- Investigate counting: sets of 5, sets of 10, sets of 2 (hands, gloves).
- Collect finger rhymes, clapping or action games and songs. Make them into a class book with photographs.
- Investigate how hands are used in prayer in different religions.

Hands

- Tools. The study of hands presents a good opportunity to introduce some research into manufacturing processes from an historical perspective.
  - Visit a museum or exhibition to study tools and implements found in your locality.
  - Make a collection of tools, old and new, to compare and contrast. Look at the way in which they are held, the materials they are made of and how they are used. (Safety warning: do not display sharp, rusty or potentially dangerous objects.) Investigate whether the tool has been replaced by a machine process today.
  - Collect pictures of old and new tools and implements: order them chronologically if possible, e.g. take a process such as writing – quills, pens, typewriters, word processors.
  - Look at tools used in the kitchen, in the garden or at school. Sort them according to function (cutters, turners, hole-makers, openers, diggers, hammers etc.), materials used etc. Study their handles – looking at insulation, grip, shape. Older children can investigate leverage.
- Invite a craftsperson to school to talk about and demonstrate a craft and the tools used, e.g. a potter, joiner, carpenter, bricklayer, silversmith, painter, blacksmith, weaver, tailor or jeweller.
- Make a collection of hand-made items, e.g. hand-knitted garments, crochet, hand-made lace, weaving, pottery, carved and hand-painted wooden articles.
- Collect stories: *The Elves and the Shoemaker*; *The Golden Axe, the Story of Chen Ping*.
- Tell the story of King Midas.
- Health and hygiene. Talk about the importance of keeping our hands clean. When do we need to clean our hands? What foods do we eat with our hands?
- Make puppets – finger puppets or glove puppets.

Families

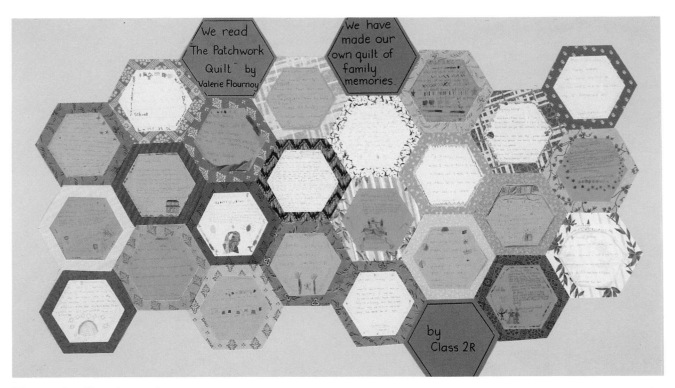

Inside the image (quilt hexagons):
"We read The Patchwork Quilt by Valerie Flournoy"
"We have made our own quilt of family memories."
"by Class 2R"

Discussion/Starting points

Any discussion in the classroom about families needs to take into account the range and diversity of family groups. A family unit (i.e. a group of people, for instance, sharing a home together, or having a common history) may consist of a large group of related people, a single parent with a child, groups of friends and relations, adopted and fostered children. Many families may be scattered geographically yet maintain very close links. Discussions could begin with talking about the special occasions when families come together, e.g. a birthday, wedding, birth of a new baby, anniversary, festivals such as Christmas, Divali, Hannukah, Eid etc. A good starting point might be to look at family parties or feasts; the sharing of food being an important component of many festivals. Most children will have much to contribute about those closest to them, and the daily experiences that they have with adults and siblings. There is a wealth of poems and stories, myths and legends that can be used as a springboard for discussions about family relationships.

Vocabulary

Kin, relations, relatives, in-laws, father, mother, parents, grandparents, grandfather, grandmother, children, offspring, twins, identical, sibling, brother, sister, stepbrother, stepsister, cousins, uncle, aunt, great-uncle, great-aunt, nephew, niece, adopted, fostered, stepfather/mother, family circle, household, maternal, paternal, generation.

Activities

- Collect a bank of family memories.
  - Read the story *Wilfred Gordon McDonald Partridge* by Mem Fox, Picture Puffin. Ask each member of your family to record a memory, maybe associated with a photograph or an object. Gather the memories to make a family album. Arrange the memories chronologically if possible.
  - Read *The Patchwork Quilt* by Valerie Flournoy/Jerry Pinkney, Picture Puffin. Make your own patchwork of memories – a collage of pictures mounted on square or hexagonal paper displayed together to make a 'patchwork quilt' (see photograph). Use contrasting colours for backing papers (maybe from wallpaper sample book) and decorate the borders of individual pieces of work.

Families

- Draw a family time line. Write about and illustrate family events.
- Match events on to the time line. Record events such as marriages, birth of children, moving house, change of jobs, children starting school, holidays, special anniversaries.
- Younger children can record family memories using a tape recorder. These can then be transcribed for them.
- Draw family members in order of height in a zig-zag book. Use a triangular-shaped piece of paper. Calculate the number of pages needed and fold the paper accordingly.

Fold to make zig-zag book. Illustrate and label.

- Make an individual word bank for names of family members and 'family' vocabulary – for each child. Make a 'doll' shape for each child – decorate with buttons, collage materials etc. Make a pocket on each shape for word lists. These can be kept in the child's drawer/tray or displayed at child height.
- Talk about different languages spoken at home. Find out how to write mother, father, sister, brother etc. in different languages (e.g. 'baji' is a name used in Punjabi for an elder sister).
- Talk about parenting and how human beings care for and raise their young. Compare with different animals and creatures. Talk about caring within the family, looking after the old and the sick. How is the birth of a baby celebrated in your family? Find out about naming ceremonies and customs associated with babies practised throughout the world. Find out about the birth of 'special' babies in different religions e.g. Jesus, Krishna, Guru Nanak, Moses. Research origins of Mother's Day or Mothering Sunday.

Brothers and sisters

Read stories and poems about siblings and brother/sister relationships.

- Make a graph. How many children in your family? Inevitably, there will be some discussion about the advantages and disadvantages of being an only child. It may be helpful to have a brainstorming session on the topic of 'Being Alone'.
- Find out about the festival of Raksha Bandhan which is celebrated in most Hindu and Sikh families. On this day, sisters give their brothers bracelets made of silver thread and decorated with gold or silver paper as a sign of love. It is also believed that the rakhris will protect the brothers from evil. The brothers give their sisters presents in return. If they live far away from each other, the gifts are sent by post.
- Talk about identical and non-identical twins.
- Discuss position in family. Read stories such as *You'll soon grow into them Titch* by Pat Hutchins, Picture Puffin, and *The Pain and the Great One* by Judy Blume, Heinemann.
- Collect photographs of brothers and sisters to display, showing relationships by matching.

Grandparents

– Talk about generations – grandparents' relationship to parents.

– Draw simple family trees to illustrate relationships (see Names). There is a range of stories , *Grandpa* by John Burningham, Puffin, *The Patchwork Quilt* by Valerie Flournoy/Jerry Pinkney, Picture Puffin, *My Grandma has Black Hair* by Mary Hoffman and Joanna Burroughes, Beaver Books, that can be used to stimulate portraits of the children's own grandparents. Old photographs can often give an insight into life in the past.

● Build up a fact file on your family. Collect data such as heights, colour of eyes, hair, handedness, favourite foods, pastimes, colours, favourite television programmes, newspapers/comics read etc. Devise a simple questionnaire to aid your data collection.

● Compare family measurements. Draw around feet or hands, measure circumference of heads, waists, wrists etc with strips of paper. Make charts by ordering strips according to length and sticking them to backing paper. Which measurements show the greatest variation?

● Write your own version of a 'Happy Families' story using the Ahlberg books, Puffin, as a starting point.

Families

- Make a family of hand-puppets or finger-puppets and write a playscript to perform.
- Make a flow diagram to tell the story of a family outing or event.
- Draw round your hand. Make each digit into a character by drawing faces. Write a story about your finger-face family.
- Investigate families and the way they lived in the past. Visit a local museum, or use fiction as a starting point. For example, a study of a Victorian family might include a consideration of their toys and games, family pastimes, where they lived, their clothes, work and transport.
- Investigate families around the world.
- Compare and contrast family life in the town with life in a rural area.

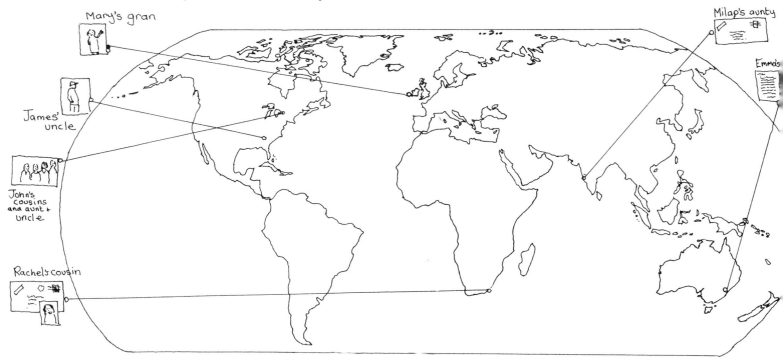

- Locate where family members live on a world map. Draw pictures or collect photographs of relatives and match them to the country where they live. Write letters to relations asking for information and photographs.

Friends

The Story of Krishna and Sudhama

Once upon a time there were two boys. One was called Krishna and the other was called Sudhama. Krishna and Sudhama were great friends. They lived in the same village in India. They would play together and look after the cattle. But Sudhama was not as strong as the other children. He was often ill, but Krishna, who was strong, was able to help his friend.

When they grew up Krishna left the village and became king. He lived with his wife in a grand palace. They were very rich, they had servants to look after them and they always had plenty to eat. Sudhama, however, had never left the village. He too married but because he was not strong he could not get work. He and his wife were very poor. They lived in a small hut and always felt hungry because they never had enough to eat.

One day, Sudhama's wife said 'Do you remember your friend Krishna? Did you know that he is now king and very rich? Why don't you go and see him and ask him if he will help us?' Sudhama wanted to see his friend again but he didn't want to go begging for help. But his wife kept going on about it so in the end, because he wanted to see Krishna, he gave in and decided to go. He wanted to take Krishna a small gift but because he was poor he couldn't afford any sweets or flowers. All he had to give was a few grains of rice.

Sudhama walked for many miles until at last he reached Krishna's palace. Sudhama explained to the servants at the palace gate that he was an old friend of Krishna's but the servants would not let him in. They did not believe that such a poor man could be a friend of the king. Fortunately however, Krishna overheard them talking and recognised Sudhama's voice. He got up from his throne and went to welcome his old friend. Then Krishna and Sudhama sat and talked for a long, long time. They remembered about when they were boys in the village and talked of all the things that they had done together. When it was time to go, Sudhama gave Krishna his small gift of rice but completely forgot to ask for help.

As he was walking home he suddenly remembered. 'Oh no,' he thought. 'My wife, she'll be so angry with me. Oh, why did I forget?' But as he walked into the village he stopped worrying about his wife because he became even more worried about something else! Their hut had completely disappeared! But in its place was a brand new house. He stopped and stared as out of the door came his wife. She was smiling. She told him all about their new home with its storerooms full of food. Sudhama smiled too because he knew that a real friend gives help without being asked.

Friends

Discussion/Starting points

Read the story of 'Krishna and Sudhama'. Talk about – How do you know if someone is your friend? What do they do? How do you show them that you are their friend? What do you do? Do you always get on with your friends? If not, why not? If you've fallen out, how do you make up?

Vocabulary

Friend, chum, pal, mate, buddy, comrade, close friend, best friend, circle of friends, friendly, helpful, kind, loving, be friends with, get on with, be fond of, care for.

Collections

Friendship stories:

> *Frog and Toad are Friends*, by Arnold Lobel, Puffin.
> *The Selfish Giant*, by Oscar Wilde.
> *The Bad Tempered Ladybird*, by Eric Carle, Picture Puffin.
> *But Martin!* by June Counsel, Faber & Faber.

Friendship poems:

> 'I Had no Friends at All' by John Kitching in *A Very First Poetry Book*, OUP.
> 'Friends' by Theresa Heine in *Another First Poetry Book* compiled by John Foster, OUP.

Activities

- Discuss the advantages and disadvantages of being alone.
- Invite some grown-ups, that the children know and like, to come and tell a true story about one of their childhood friendships.
- You will need a camera and some film (and a flash if possible). Ask each child to write down his or her own name and a list of friends' names. It is important that this is done without discussion amongst the children. The list may have only two names on it, that of you and your best friend, or you may want to list lots of friends. Remind the children about friends in other classes. Ask them to write down where they would like to be photographed – select a location somewhere in the school grounds! Ask the children also to decide whether they want just their face (taken in profile or facing the camera) or their whole body or whether sitting or standing. It is well worth the time letting each child make these decisions as it will result in a very varied set of photographs. Each child can use the developed photograph as a stimulus for writing about their friends.
- Make some 'Guess Who?' cards – fold a piece of A4 card in half keeping the crease at the top. On the front write some clues about your friend, and write 'Guess Who?' at the bottom. Lift the flap and draw an accurate picture of your friend. Pin the cards to the wall for others to read.
- Re-tell or re-write a favourite story substituting your best friend for the main character, for example, 'Juan and the Beanstalk', 'Sandeep and the Seven Dwarves', 'Glenys and the Three Bears'.
- Make enlarged photocopies of the 'Start a Story' cards that are printed on the next page. Cut and mount on to card then cover with transparent self-adhesive film. Instruct the children to start a story by copying a card and inserting their friends' names in the gaps. Complete the story in draft and then re-draft or edit as necessary. Produce the final draft as a book. Dedicate it to your friends and give it to them to read.
- Make additional 'Start a Story' cards that include references to local place names or topical happenings.

**** and **** had forgotten their books, so they went back to school to get them. As they walked into the playground they saw a man stealing the school video. **** shouted.....

* * * * and * * * * were walking down the street. Suddenly, a blue hand came out of a dustbin and it .....

* * * * and * * * * were playing in the playground when something very odd happened. They both became invisible. The teacher....

**** and **** went to a museum. They were looking at the dinosaur skeleton when it suddenly came alive. The skeleton began to.......

* * * * and * * * * were walking down the street. They found a purse on the road. It had twenty pounds in it. * * * * Said......

* * * * and * * * * were playing in the park when a big dog ran up to them. * * * * started to.....

* * * * and * * * * were using the computer. The screen was blank. * * * * was about to press one of the keys when a message appeared on the screen. It said.....

* * * * and * * * * came to school very early one morning. They saw a spaceship in the playground. They went up to it and.....

Sharing

Discussion/Starting points

Bring a banana to school. Select two children to help you act out the story of The Monkeys and the Banana. The children are to be the two young monkeys. (But remember not to tell this story after a full meal because *you* are about to eat the banana!)

The Monkeys and the Banana

Once upon a time two young monkeys found a banana. The little monkeys were greedy and began to quarrel because they both wanted to eat it. After a while an older monkey came by and looked hungrily at the banana. After a while she said, 'Little ones, why are you quarrelling? To be fair you should share the banana. Here, let me break it in half for you.' The older monkey took the banana, carefully peeled back the skin, split it in two and held up the pieces. 'Oh dear,' she said, 'one piece is larger than the other.' So she broke a bit off the larger piece and ate it. She held up the pieces again 'Oh dear,' she said, 'now the other piece is bigger.' So she broke off another bit and popped it in her mouth. The two little monkeys watched, not realising what was happening. The cunning old monkey carried on doing this and the pieces became smaller and smaller until there was only one tiny piece left. Quickly she gobbled this up and scampered away laughing. The two little monkeys sat and stared at each other. They realised how they had been fooled and how silly they had been to quarrel. Because they had been so greedy they were now left with nothing.

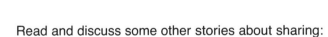

Read and discuss some other stories about sharing:

King Jahangir and the baby (when sharing is not the best option) by Indu Anand, André Deutsch with Jennie Ingham Associates Ltd.

Little Red Hen (sharing the work load)

The Stork and the Fox (Aesop's fable about sharing a meal)

Tiddalick, the Frog who caused a Flood (sharing the resources in the environment) by Robert Roennfeldt, Picture Puffin.

'Everybody said no!' by Sheila Lavelle, slightly abridged version in *Tinderbox*, A & C Black, (sharing the work load).

Vocabulary

Share out, divide up, measure out, weigh out, go halves, go fifty-fifty, take part, join in, have a say in, share and share alike, take the good with the bad, pull one's weight, take turns; whole, fraction, half, quarter, part, portion, piece, slice, equal, fair share, unequal, unfair, full, half-full, empty, half-empty, remainder, left over, spare.

Activities

● Talk about the classroom space, its books and resources as things that have to be shared by all who use them. Discuss sharing the responsibility for making sure that everything is kept in good condition and left tidy for the next person.

● Discuss sharing the world and its resources. Talk about the great variety of life on the earth and how we must care for the planet and all its life forms.

Sharing

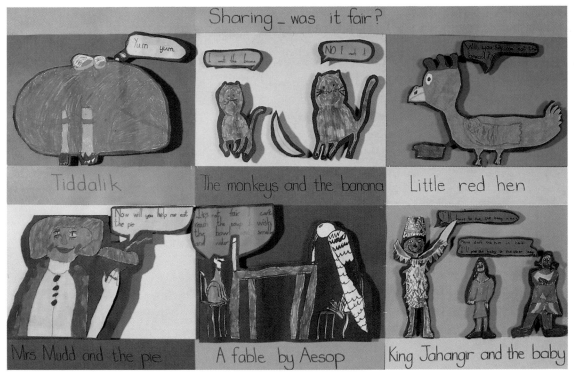

Sharing stories: mount the cut-out drawings on black paper and trim, leaving a border. To create a 3D effect, glue tubes or small boxes behind the figures.

- Give the children a variety of things to be divided into two equal parts:
  - a lump of Plasticine
  - a length of string
  - a sheet of paper
  - a bottle of water (provide two clear beakers)
  - a pile of wooden bricks.

  How do you know that the two parts are equal? How could you check? Always display the whole unit alongside the two halves so that the children can compare them.

- Fold a sheet of paper in half, then in half again. Unfold the paper. In the top left-hand section draw your best friend and in the top right-hand section draw yourself. Take a handful of Unifix cubes, count them and write down the number. Now share the cubes out between you and your friend, placing them below the pictures you have drawn. Did they share out equally or have you got one left over? Note what happened. Repeat this a few times. Look at which numbers you were able to share equally and which numbers left you with one over.

- Play the Fair Share Game; a sharing game for four players. You will need sixty-nine 1p coins, a set of small cards numbered 1–18 placed in a container, three cards with 'yes' written on one side and 'no' on the other. One child is the banker with the money and the numbered cards. The banker selects a card and each of the other players has to predict whether that given number of 1p coins would share equally amongst the three of them. They make their predictions with the 'yes' or 'no' cards. The banker then shares out the given number of coins. The players whose predictions were correct get to keep a coin each, the remainder of the money being returned to the banker. The game continues until all numbered cards have been drawn by the banker. The winner is the child with the highest number of correct predictions and hence the one with the most 1p coins.

- Cut some fruit and vegetables in half but be selective as some have more visual interest than others, e.g. pomegranates, kiwi fruit, figs, red cabbage. Make drawings of the cross sections. Weigh the two halves on balance scales to see if they are of equal weight.

Penfriends

Pre-arrangements

When selecting another school with a parallel class for your children to write to, consider the following issues:

- How often do you think the children will be writing to each other?
- How will this integrate with the rest of the curriculum?
- Can the other teacher enable her children to match this commitment?
- Are you looking for a school that is nearby so that the classes can easily visit each other during the year?
- Will the children just be exchanging letters or will they be writing books for each other and exchanging pieces of craft work?
- Do you think the children should exchange letters with others from similar backgrounds or different backgrounds?
- Should they write to children overseas?
- Children frequently produce some of their best 'work' for their penfriends. Are you going to arrange for them to show it to their parents before it gets sent off?
- If the class sizes are unequal, are there children at one end who are willing to share the same penfriend and at the other end are there those willing to write to more than one penpal?

Having made these decisions and found a class to write to, it is time to launch the penfriend project!

Cranford Infant School,
Berkeley Avenue,
Cranford,
Hounslow,
TW4 6LB.

.... September, 1992

Dear Penfriend,

My name is ....
I am .... years old.
My birthday is on ....
I live at ....
....
I live with ....
I go to .... School.
At school I like to ....
At playtime I play with ....
I would like to be your penfriend.
Please write back soon.
Love from ....

Discussion/Starting points

Talk about friends, new friends, penfriends. Show the children on a map where their penfriends live. Explain about sending letters and about getting them back. Start the correspondence with a proforma letter. This first letter can be sent with a photograph or a self-portrait. The receiving teacher allocates the letters and the children can reply using a similar format. It simplifies the organisation for both teachers, and alleviates any possible disappointment for the children, if the teachers reply on behalf of any absentees.

Vocabulary

Penfriend, penpal, letter, card, postcard, send, receive, post, postbox, letterbox, postman, postwoman, collection, sorting office, franking machine, deliver, stamp; find out, discover, get to know, learn all about.

Collections

Writing paper, headed school stationery, envelopes, stamps; books about the postal service; books, pictures, artefacts etc. that relate to where the penfriends live.

Penfriends

Activities

- Before opening your letter, think what you want to know about your penfriend. Now open the letter and read it. Has your penfriend told you what you want to know? If not, why not ask your questions in your next letter?
- Enter the penfriends' birthdays in the class diary.
- Send your penfriend
  - a postcard
  - a card for Christmas, Divali, Easter, Eid or Hannukah
  - a happy New Year card
  - a birthday card.
- Draft a story for your penfriend. Make it into a book and dedicate it to your penfriend.
- Make a class book for your penfriends. It could be about your school, your country or your local area.
- Get each child to write his or her name on a separate strip of paper. Now ask the children to arrange their names in alphabetical order pasting them down the lefthand side of a large sheet of paper. Then ask them to write down their penfriends' names but to paste these strips in alphabetical order down the righthand side. Ask them to match their names to those of their penfriends.
- Make a time line to show the months in the year. Use this to plan and record what has been sent and received.
- Find out about where your penfriend lives by asking questions or using reference books.
- If you are going to visit your penfriend, mark out the route you will be taking.
- Send your penfriend an invitation to visit you. Prepare a tea party.

Homes

Discussion/Starting points

What makes your home a special place for you? Talk about feelings associated with going home. What do you look forward to doing? Who do you look forward to seeing? Have a class or group 'brain-storming' session. Write words associated with 'home' on house-shaped charts.

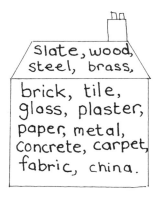

my home is.....
warm, safe, dry, comfortable, cosy, noisy, crowded, happy, bright.

slate, wood, steel, brass, brick, tile, glass, plaster, paper, metal, concrete, carpet, fabric, china.

attic, bedroom, bathroom, office, hall, study, sitting room, dining room, kitchen, utility room, playroom, conservatory.

Do you have a favourite place in your home? Do you have a place full of your favourite things? Read *When I'm Sleepy* by Jane R. Howard and illustrated by Lynne Cherry, Beaver Books. Imagine what it would be like to sleep in different places. Have you ever stayed the night away from home? Did you take anything with you to remind you of home? Read *A House is a House for me*, by Mary Ann Hoberman, illustrated by Betty Fraser, Picture Puffin. Can you add to this list of homes? Try to think of some rhymes and alliterations.

Vocabulary

Animal homes: hive, nest, coop, sty, fold, barn, kennel, hutch, stable, lair, den, hole, burrow, warren, earth, sett, drey, eyrie, perch etc; dwelling, habitat, residence, lodgings, digs, homestead, urban, rural, flats, castle, penthouse, maisonette, apartment, chalet, bungalow, mansion, manor, farm, houseboat, mobile home, caravan, tent, cottage, villa, detached, semi-detached, terraced.

Collections

Samples of building materials e.g. bricks, slates, wood; decorating materials e.g. fabric, carpet and wallpaper samples; pictures of houses/homes; descriptions of homes from local estate agents.

Activities

- Go on an 'I-Spy' walk in the local area to look at homes. Teachers should prepare a simple questionnaire for children to record their observations.
- How can you tell how old a home is? Visit some old houses/homes in the area. Can you find any clues to show how the people used to live in the past? Can you find out how the home was heated? How did they cook? Wash? Where did they sleep? Look for signs of age. Has the home been adapted for modern day living? How?
- Study building materials. Look closely at how materials are used in your home for different purposes. Make a list. Look at brick patterns, shapes of roofs, types of windows and doors. Investigate how homes are kept warm and dry. Look at systems and services, e.g. water, waste disposal, electricity, gas heating, ventilation.
- Investigate animal homes.
- Read *The Town Mouse and the Country Mouse*. Discuss and compare life in urban and rural areas. Studies could involve a comparison of contrasting areas (see Penfriends).

Homes

- Match children's names to a map of the local area. Ordnance Survey maps scale 1:1200 allow the pinpointing of house numbers in urban areas. Display pictures of homes matched to the map with ribbons or string to each child's name, address and picture (as shown in the photograph). Lift the flap to reveal who lives here!

- Maths Activities
  - Investigate house numbers – odds and evens.
  - Look at shapes of windows and the arrangement of panes.
  - Collect data, e.g. colour of front doors, number of rooms, number of windows, number of doors, and make graphs.
  - Investigate tessellating shapes. Which shape would you use to tile your wall or floor?
  - Make a house-shape puzzle (as shown in the photograph).

- Write your name and address. Write a letter to somebody at home.

- Make a classbook based on *The Jolly Postman* by Allan Ahlberg, Heinemann. Design the pages so that letters can be inserted into envelopes.

- Write a story: 'Through my window I can see . . .'
  Illustrate – Draw view from window
  and cut out a frame. Use a template to draw window panes.
  Glue window frame over picture of view.

Draw a view.

Make a frame from coloured paper, using a template.

- Design and write about your 'dream house'.

- Make model homes using junk materials. Can you make a door that opens?

- Build a high-rise block of flats using shoeboxes. Each child designs and makes the interior of individual flats using wallpaper and fabric samples, together with junk materials.

- Print pictures of homes using construction toys and building blocks.

- Make a collection of rubbings of building materials found in your home. Make a book.

Then and Now

Discussion/Starting points

- Ask the children to find out where they were born. Also, ask each child to find out about the birth place of their mother or father and of one grandparent. Record the information on three adhesive labels.

 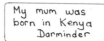 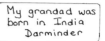

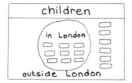 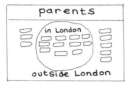 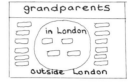

- These labels can then be stuck on to three charts, each with the local area marked in the centre.

- This information can then be presented as a Carroll chart.

birthplace	children	parents	grandparents
in London	20	17	4
outside London	5	8	15

- Make flag labels to mark the different places of birth on a map of the U.K. and a map of the world.

Grenada   Jamaica   Eire   Scotland

- At the same time start a photograph collection of the three generations:
  - photographs of us now
  - photographs of our parents when they were children
  - photographs of our grandparents when they were children
  - encourage the children to look for differences in the photographs e.g. colour versus black and white photography, clothes, footwear etc.

Vocabulary

Now, the present, modern, up-to-date, then, the past, history, long ago, within living memory, beyond living memory, ancient, dated, out-of-date, ancestor, descendant.

Collections

Pictures, books and artefacts that illustrate the domestic life of the three periods under study (the present; within living memory; and a particular period selected, because of local interest, beyond living memory).

Activities

- Ask the children to list their top ten favourite foods. Each child can then take the list home for an adult to complete (see facing page). Discuss with the children which foods seem to be 'new' e.g. pizza, kiwi fruit, etc.

Then and Now

My name is	parent / grandparent (please delete)
my favourite foods	Did you eat these when you were a child?
pizza ice cream spaghetti chips baked beans crisps yoghurt sausages fruit burgers	

- Collect new and 'old style' packaging. Talk about how shopping has changed over the years.
- Ask the children to list all the machines that are in their homes and to find out how things used to be done without some of these machines. Each child can then take the list home for an adult to complete.

My name is	parent / grandparent (please delete)
Machines in my home.	Did you have these when you were a child?
microwave electric kettle fridge food mixer washing machine vacuum cleaner tumble dryer	

Machines you can buy today	Machines our parents remember	Machines our grandparents remember
electric cooker microwave video tumble dryer vacuum cleaner		

Collect this information on a class chart.

- Invite a parent and a grandparent into the classroom to talk about their respective childhood memories and to answer the children's questions.
- Having compared the children's lives with those within living memory, pose the question: How can we find out about the way children lived long, long before your grandparents were born?
- The location of the school will determine how best to extend this study further. If there is a local museum, historical site or heritage centre nearby – then use the 'key' period represented as the basis for a mini-project. If no such resources are available, then contact your local library or local history society. They may be able to help by providing books or a speaker who could answer the children's questions.
  Discuss:
  – how we live now
  – what life was like for our parents and grandparents when they were children
  – children's lives from a selected period of history beyond living memory.

Famous people

Discussion/Starting points

What does 'being famous' mean? Have you ever met a famous person? Tell us about it. What do you think it would be like to be famous? Can you think of any advantages or disadvantages? Read *The Magic Lamp* by Jeff Brown, Mammoth. Can you name a famous person who is alive today? What is this person famous for? How do you know about this person? Talk about the media, television, radio, newspapers and magazines. Talk about the kind of things that someone might be famous for e.g. sport, politics, music, singing, dance, art, an act of heroism, acting in a popular television series etc. What would you like to be famous for? Some people are famous and were famous because of their family connections. Talk about royal families. Talk about famous kings and queens from history.

Vocabulary

Famous, infamous, heroic, distinguished, celebrated, renowned, esteemed, honoured, celebrity, public figure, eminent, important, prestigious, notorious, publicity, limelight, spotlight, stardom, champion, 'in the public eye'.

Activities

- Write the history of a chosen famous person. Sequence the events of the person's life and draw a flow diagram. Dramatise the life history by using the *This is Your Life* format.
- Imagine what it would be like to be 'famous for a day' and write a story about your experiences.
- Study portraits of famous people in a local art gallery or museum. These pictures often contain clues as to why the people were famous – they may be portrayed carrying out an activity, they might be wearing special clothes, or there might be artefacts. Paint or draw a portrait of a famous person putting clues into the picture to show why the person is famous.
- Write a newspaper report about an heroic deed. Find out about people who have been recognised for their bravery in the past. How are heroic deeds recognised and commemorated? e.g. awards, medals, plaques and memorials.
- Talk about and distinguish between real people and fictional characters.
- Research the lives of important people in the great religions of the world, e.g. Jesus, Buddha, the Prophet Muhammad, together with people of faith such as Guru Nanak, St. Francis, Gandhi.
- Look at the accounts of history or diaries written by famous people.
- Research the life of a famous person in history and look at how his/her life differs from yours.
- Find out about famous people who lived in your area. Visit a local museum or contact a local historical society for information. Have you ever seen any plaques on buildings to show that someone famous lived there? Research the names of local streets, parks and large houses to find out whether there is any connection with an important historical figure or family.
- Ask your parents about people who were famous when they were at school. Ask your grandparents about the celebrities that they can remember. Collect pictures and memorabilia.
- Find out about famous people associated with a particular topic or area of study. For example, trace the people involved in the history of aviation. Sequence events in chronological order and make an illustrated time-line.
- Find out about famous people associated with your school.

Famous People

old necklace

black rug wool

black plastic flowerpot

milk bottle tops and fruit gums

crêpe paper leaves on wire

paper doilies

glued-on tapioca and lentils

padding underneath full skirt

painted cardboard stomacher on ribbons or velcro

beaded bag

jumble sale 'crêpe' dress

pleated or striped skirt with gold-painted flowers

piece of sheeting with felt-tip purple stripe

Children will enjoy dressing up as famous people.

- Write letters to famous people. Discuss and formulate the questions you would like to ask them about their lives. Famous people are very busy. To avoid the risk of individual children being disappointed, send class or group letters to several famous people.
- During an arts festival or book week, arrange for a famous author or illustrator to visit your school.
- Make a collection and a display of books by a favourite author, together with autobiographies and biographies.
- Paint pictures of television personalities and frame them with a pretend screen.
- Organise a whole school or class dressing-up day. Children can dress as their favourite famous person from the past or present.

Famous People might not be undertaken as a topic in itself, but might be the focus for a whole-school theme, led by a series of assemblies, with each class contributing elements that are relevant to their individual class topics. For example, a class studying 'Journeys' as their topic might contribute research into famous explorers or aviators, or a class studying a festival might contribute a profile of a religious leader or an historical figure e.g. Guy Fawkes.

Journeys

Discussion/Starting points

Design a questionnaire for the children to complete to find out about their travels.

Have you ever been on a journey?   YES/NO

Please tick the boxes that show how you have travelled.

by aeroplane	☐	by canoe	☐	by horse	☐
by bicycle or tricycle	☐	by car	☐	by hovercraft	☐
by boat	☐	by coach	☐	by mini-cab	☐
by bus	☐	by donkey	☐	by taxi	☐
by camel	☐	by helicopter	☐	by walking	☐

Please write down any other ways ....

Think about the longest journey that you have gone on.

Where did you go to? ....

How did you travel? ....

With whom did you travel ....

Did you sleep there?   YES/NO

What did you do there? ....

Have you ever been to any other countries?   YES/NO

If yes, which countries have you visited? ....

Name three places that you would like to visit ....

Now get the children to administer the questionnaire to their parents or members of the school staff. The children can then work in pairs and go through the completed questionnaires, to find out, for example, how many people have travelled by car or camel. This information can be represented on a bar graph.

Vocabulary

Journey, travel, tour, see the world, globetrot, explore, discover, move, go places, sightsee, set sail, put to sea, set out, go forth, migrate, visit, wend one's way, tread a path, follow the road, march on; go on a . . . trip, safari, trek, voyage, pilgrimage; travellers: explorer, adventurer, voyager, spaceman or woman, astronaut, pilgrim, hajji, walker, hiker, rambler, trekker, globetrotter, tourist, sightseer, holidaymaker, passenger, rider, driver, cyclist, motorcyclist, sailor, navigator; journey's end, destination, end of the road, faraway, distant, overseas, abroad, near, close to home, homeward bound, local.

Collections

Atlases – geographic and road, an A to Z of the nearest city; maps – local ordnance survey, county or borough map, map of the U.K., world maps (pictorial, relief and political), London underground map, a local street map, a star map; globes – relief and political, aerial photographs, compasses, a suitcase, travel bag and backpack, travel brochures, tickets, expired passports, luggage labels, reference books about different countries; models or pictures of aeroplanes, trains, boats, ships, buses, coaches, cars, bicycles, horses, camels, etc.; books about transport; collections of holiday souvenirs and postcards.

Journeys

Terminal 3 at Cranford Infant School.

Activities

- Think about your journey to school. Draw a map to illustrate your route. Begin with a picture of your home, then draw the road or pathway that you follow. Draw the things that you pass on the way and end with a picture of the school.
- Make a bar graph to show how the children travel to school.
- In the play corner set up one of the following:
  - an airport with baggage check-in, passport control, an airport shop selling postcards, magazines, newspapers, sweets, etc., and aeroplane seating
  - a travel agency with brochures and tickets
  - a boat for Max's journey to the Land of the Wild Things.
- Use a compass to locate north, south, east and west in the classroom. Ask the child with the compass to point to the north and get another child to place a 'north' label at the most northerly part of the room. Repeat for south, west and east. Then go to the playground and label the perimeter of the playground in the same way.

Journeys

<boys' toilets|

<library|

|office>

- Collect place names with north, south, east and west in them, for example, Northumberland, Southampton, East Ham, the West Indies etc.

- Make some direction signs for the school. Place these outside the classroom exit point and at subsequent corners. The children can then work in pairs, one child selecting a destination and the partner giving instructions in terms of going straight on or turning right or left in order to reach the destination. Alternatively, a pair of children can plan a route by writing down the directions and another pair could follow their instructions and discover the mystery destination.

- Take a felt-tip pen on a journey.
  - Using 1 cm squared or dotted paper, take a felt-tip pen for a journey – your felt-tip can only travel along the lines. It cannot take a shortcut across squares or cut corners. Travel all over the paper and end up where you began.
  - Using 1 cm squared or dotted paper, take your felt-tip pen on a new journey following these special directions. 'Start in the top left-hand corner. Go down two centimetres. Now turn right and go along for two centimetres. Now go up two centimetres. Turn left and go along for two centimetres.' Follow this 'square' journey with similar instructions so that squares and oblongs of varying dimensions are produced. As the children become more confident make the instructions more demanding. Always remember to make your own 'route map' so the children can compare the end results with the original. Let the children take turns in giving the directions.

- Programme a Turtle or a Roamer to move and change directions.

- Contrast these straight line routes with journeys that meander about. Using a roller, spread some paint across a large sheet of Perspex or Formica. Ask a child to trace a path in the paint, using his or her index finger. The path must never be straight but twist and turn around and about. When a curved, wavy and convoluted route has been created, take a print by placing a sheet of paper across the paint. Use a dry roller across the paper if necessary.

- Give directions in movement lessons that require the children to turn right or left, or go straight ahead, or to twist and turn.

- Think about the 'journeys' made by things rather than people.
  - The journey of an empty crisp packet from the litter bin to the dump. Some children might like to interview the school caretaker.
  - The journey of a letter from sender to receiver. Perhaps the school postman or woman would spare a few minutes to answer some questions.
  - The journey of a house martin from Great Britain to Africa. Identify land and sea areas on a map.

- Talk about the idea of life as a journey. What are the important milestones that children pass?

- Read stories or poems where a journey is the central theme:
  The Israelites' Flight from Egypt (see chapter on Pesach).
  Where the Wild Things Are by Maurice Sendak, Picture Puffin.
  Whatever Next by Jill Murphy, Picturemac.
  The Owl and the Pussycat by Edward Lear.
  James and the Giant Peach by Roald Dahl, Puffin.

Walkabout

The travel agency offered plenty of opportunities for role play.

Pre-arrangements

Obtain a large scale map or street plan of the locality immediately around the school. Decide how many times it will be possible for you to arrange for small groups to go on local visits. Each group will visit a building of local interest. Try to select buildings that contrast in age or function or construction. Contact the necessary individuals in advance to arrange these visits, for example, the bank manager, the priest, the supermarket manager etc.

Discussion/Starting points

What is a building? Is the school a building? Is a flat a building? Is the park a building? Is a bus shelter a building? Having established what a building is, brainstorm as many different types of building as you can. Record the list of buildings for display and also provide each child with a copy of the list to use on a clipboard.

Take all the children on a walkabout of the local neighbourhood ensuring that they pass by the pre-selected buildings as well as many others. Ask them to tick off buildings from their list as they see them. Photograph these buildings and any others that are of interest.

Vocabulary

Neighbourhood, nearby, close by, area, parish, local – plus all the words to describe local landscape features, buildings etc.

Collections

Sets of objects that relate to the local buildings visited by the children; photographs, prints, books that show what the area used to look like.

Activities

- Talk about the route the children followed and mark it out on the local map. When the photographs are developed place these on the map.
- Re-read the original brain-storming list and mark off the buildings that were seen. Add any new buildings to the list.

Walkabout

- Ask the children to select one of the buildings that they saw and do a detailed pencil drawing of it, adding colour with thin water-based inks. Alternatively, paint a picture using powder paints and, when it is dry, add details using a felt-tip pen.

- Now focus in on the group visits to the selected buildings. Firstly, work out a general question-naire with the whole class that would be appropriate for all the groups to use; then see if the class has any specific questions that they want a particular group to investigate. Immediately after each group returns from its visit, ask them to relate to the rest of the class what they did and what they saw. Ask them to label and display any objects that they have obtained, make models of the building and write down all they know about it. Remind them to write 'thank you' letters too.

- Decide which of the buildings visited had the greatest potential for role play, and set up the play corner appropriately.

- Talk about what else the children saw locally apart from the buildings.

- Look in the Highway Code. Which of the road safety signs were seen? What do they mean? Create some safety signs for the school.

- Make a book of local road names (see illustration). On each lefthand page write the road names and on each righthand page write down the following: Avenue, Close, Crescent, Drive, Gardens, Grove, Lane, Park, Road, Street etc. Can you pair the pages to make a local road sign?

- Find out about the history of local place names.

- Invite a local resident who has lived in the neighbourhood for many years to come and tell the children about how the area has changed. Support this talk with old photographs, prints, books etc.

- Talk about any open spaces, fields, gardens, parks, canals, streams, ponds, landscape features etc. that are in the neighbourhood and locate these on the map. Design posters that feature the country code or that focus on the dangers of playing near open water or railway tracks.

- Discuss what it is about the neighbourhood that makes it a nice place to live in. Then talk about the things that the children do not like. How would they improve the area? Present these suggestions in a class book and arrange for a local planning officer or councillor to visit the school so that the children can discuss their ideas.

Special Places

Create a special place for quiet reading.

Discussion/Starting points

When is it very noisy in school? When is it very quiet in school? Which is the noisiest part of the school? Which is the quietest part? Let's write your suggestions down. Let's go very quietly to all of these places and listen to find out what we can hear.

Write down across the top of a large sheet of paper the areas that the class visited. Under each heading write down the different sounds that the children heard. Decide which was the noisiest place. Was it the place with the most sounds or just one or two very loud sounds? Which was the quietest place? Was it completely silent or were there some sounds?

Vocabulary

Noisy, busy, crowded, bustling, hustling, humming, lively, coming and going, rushing to and fro, rushed off one's feet, busy as a bee; special, favourite, preferred, private, quiet, peaceful, calm, tranquil, hushed, silent, secluded, empty, not a sound, not a squeak, so quiet you can hear a pin drop.

Collections

Postcards, prints, photographs, books etc. that depict special places: natural wild places, gardens, famous buildings, places of pilgrimage etc; mementoes or souvenirs from special places that the children have visited.

Activities

* Create a 'silent reading area' for those children who are seeking a peaceful and uninterrupted read. Use screens or a playhouse frame to create an enclosed space. Use drapes (old saris are ideal) or strips of crêpe paper to make an awning. The area should not contain books or resources that other children might need access to, and it will be necessary to define the number of users at any one time. (See photograph above.)

Special places

- Do you like it best when it's noisy or quiet? What do you like to do when it's quiet? Read *The Grass House* by Shirley Hughes.

The Grass House
The grass house
Is my private place.
Nobody can see me
In the grass house.
Feathery plumes
Meet over my head.
Down here,
In the green, there are:
Seeds
Weeds
Stalks
Pods
And tiny flowers.

Only the cat
And some busy, hurrying ants
Know where my grass house is.

Shirley Hughes

(from *Out and About* by Shirley Hughes, Walker Books, London, 1988.)

- Read *Peace at last* by Jill Murphy, Picturemac, and *Five Minutes' Peace*, also by Jill Murphy, Walker Books. What does your mum do when she wants a bit of peace and quiet?
- What do you do and where do you go to when you feel sad? What about your brothers and sisters? What do they do? Where do they go?
- Ask a pair of children to draw a large sketch map of the playground showing any playground equipment, markings, seats etc. Each child can then make a pipecleaner model of himself/herself with a small name card attached to each. These can then be glued (using strong glue) on to their favourite area on the playground plan. Each child can write about the reasons for their choice and this writing can be displayed around the plan.
- Think of all the different places that you have been to. Which place did you like the best? Why?
- Draw a detailed picture of your favourite place to show everyone, especially if they've never been there themselves, exactly what it is like. Create a picture frame from strips of card. Print a pattern on the frame or use collage materials for your pattern. The frame will show everyone that your picture is of a very special place.
- Invite into class some visitors who have made some very special journeys. Is there a parent or relative who has visited the Golden Temple or the Taj Mahal, or been to Jerusalem? Has anyone made a pilgrimage to Lourdes or Mecca? Maybe someone has travelled back to the country of their birth.
- Encourage children to think of special events in people's lives and then to think where events such as naming ceremonies, weddings etc. take place. Follow this up with a visit to a local place of worship.

Cycles

Make a class 'tadpole' book.

Discussion/Starting points

What is a cycle? Talk about the concept of circular progression in terms of life-cycles, the rain cycle, night and day, days of the week, months of the year. Refer to classroom rotas and timetables. Talk about wheels and circles.

Vocabulary

Circle, revolve, revolution, rotate, come round again, orbit, circuit; life-cycle, egg, larva, pupa, metamorphosis, develop, change, grow, nymph, spawn, tadpole, chrysalis, caterpillar, water-cycle, evaporate, water vapour, droplet, tropical rainforest, desert, climate, condensation, drought; lunar cycle, annual, anniversary.

Collections

Wheels, calendars, timetables, a globe, circular items; items that can be re-cycled; things made from re-cycled paper.

Activities

Life-cycles

- Talk about the stages of different life-cycles e.g.
  - egg, larva, pupa, adult (butterfly)
  - egg, young adult, adult (worm)
  - egg, nymph, adult (dragonfly).

  Study one life-cycle in particular e.g. the life-cycle of the frog.

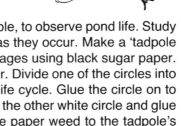

- Find out about the life-cycle of the frog. Visit a local pond, if possible, to observe pond life. Study the development of tadpoles. Keep a diary, noting the changes as they occur. Make a 'tadpole book' as shown in the photograph. Cut out the tadpole-shaped pages using black sugar paper. Fan-pleat the tail of the tadpole. Cut out two circles of white paper. Divide one of the circles into quarters by folding, and draw and label the stages of the frog's life cycle. Glue the circle on to the body of the tadpole. Write a story about a frog or a tadpole on the other white circle and glue it on to the other side of the tadpole shape. Glue or staple crêpe paper weed to the tadpole's 'mouth'. Hang the individual tadpoles on a line across the classroom or make a book with the pages.

41

- Read the story *Tiddalick, the Frog who caused a Flood* by Robert Roennfeldt, Puffin.
  - Make pictures of Tiddalick, the giant-sized frog, using wax resist. Crayon a large Tiddalick, pressing firmly with wax crayons, and then paint with a thin wash of blue fluorescent paint.
  - Tell the story of Tiddalick by drawing a cartoon strip.
  - Dramatise the story of Tiddalick.
  - What makes you laugh? Collect jokes and funny stories and make a *Tiddalick Joke Book*.
  - Collect as many stories as you can about frogs.
  - Make a 'turn the wheel' card – as shown in the illustration.

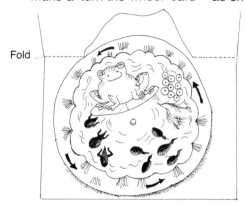 

Fold

The Rain Cycle

Why do we need rain? Read the story *Bringing the Rain to Kapiti Plain* by Verna Aardema, Picturemac. Talk about the importance of rain and the uses of water. Discuss the effects of water shortage and also the damage caused by flooding. Look at the areas of the world that receive the most rainfall and those that receive the least. Study maps and globes to find oceans, seas, lakes and rivers. Find out about the different kinds of clouds.

Describe the stages of the water-cycle.

- The water in rivers, oceans, lakes and seas is heated by the sun.
- As it warms the water evaporates and rises into the air as water vapour.
- The vapour cools and turns back into water.
- Then the water falls as rain and snow and the cycle starts all over again.
  Make a large wall story to illustrate the rain cycle.

Time

- Write 'days of the week' stories. Read *On Friday Something Funny Happened* by John Prater, Picture Puffin, or *Mr. Wolf's Week* by Colin Hawkins, Picture Puffin.
- Make a class timetable depicting the week's activities. Which things do we do everyday? Which activities do we do once a week?
- Make a class calendar for the school year. Enter all the children's birthdays. Talk about the annual events, the anniversaries of historical events, festivals, holidays and celebrations.
- Find out about the seasons, and the movement of the earth around the sun.
- Investigate the lunar cycle. See the chapter on Ramadan and Eid-ul-Fitr.
- Illustrate the morning-afternoon-evening-night cycle on a circle of paper divided into quarters.
- Find out about the Chinese New Year cycle. What year are we in now? In which year were you born?

Re-cycling

Find out about materials that can be recycled. Talk about the importance of preserving the earth's precious resources. Investigate a scheme operating in your area and participate in the collection of materials.

New Year

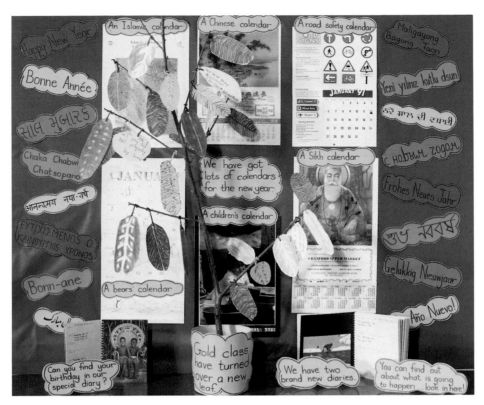

Discussion/Starting points

Make a New Year's Tree. Talk about New Year's resolutions and 'turning over a new leaf'. Ask the children if they have made any resolutions or if anyone in their family has. Talk about how they can try to do something completely new, or try to stop a bad old habit. Ask the children to write their New Year's resolutions on the reverse side of the leaves then attach them with pipecleaners to the branches of the New Year's Tree (a bare branch firmly secured in a pot – see photograph).

Vocabulary

End, close, finish, over and done with, final, last, bring to an end, bring down the curtains, put up the shutters, shut up shop, wind up, close down, call it a day, cut off, halt, stop; begin, make a start, start out, fire away, kick off, strike up, begin at the beginning, start from scratch, make a fresh start, turn over a new leaf.

Collections

A variety of calendars and diaries for the new year; calendars that display one month at a time, three months at a time, those that have the days arranged in week blocks, those that list the days one under each other, a year's wall planner etc; calendars that represent different cultures – these can be obtained from some of the international relief charities, international airlines or businesses run by members of ethnic communities.

Activities

- Talk about things that might happen in the new year. Make a chart for either the class or a group of children to complete.
    - things that I think will definitely happen
    - things that I think might happen
    - things that I would like to happen but probably won't.

Monitor these predictions throughout the year, or review them at the end of the school year. Have they happened, might they still happen or do you know that they won't happen?

New Year

- Talk about New Year traditions, including Hogmanay, and read Ian Serraillier's poem 'First Foot', from *Let's Celebrate, Festival Poems*, OUP.

> **First Foot**
>
> One . . . two . . . three . . . four . . .
> Midnight knocking on our door
>
> A tall dark stranger waits outside
> Turning away, his face to hide.
>
> A lump of coal in one black hand –
> What does it mean? Why does he stand?
>
> Holding his other hand out to us all
> As we welcome him into the midnight hall?
>
> Goodbye to the old year, good luck in the new,
> 'Come in, dear friend, peace be with you.'
>
> Ian Serraillier

- Talk about making wishes for the future. What sort of things do the children wish for? Talk about the poor, the homeless and the hungry. What sort of things do the children think these people wish for? Read them the story of the Old Woman who lived in a Vinegar Bottle, and the story of King Midas.

Discuss these stories.

- Construct time lines:
  - Make a time line that shows the school year. Mark on the children's birthdays and other key events. Make labels for the past and the future and an arrow for the present. Ask someone to adjust 'the present' label each day.
  - Make a time line that starts with the year in which the children were born and continues on up to the year that they will leave the school. Make past, present and future labels.

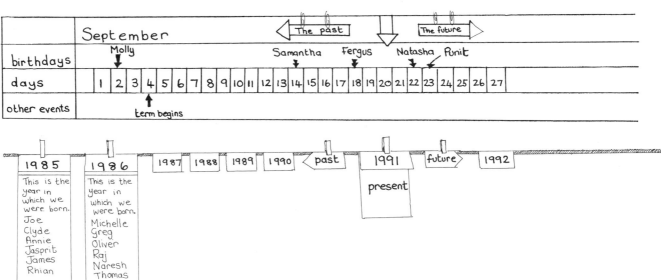

New Year

- Set up an 'Old and New' table with pairs of objects.

- Talk about the past, the present and the future. Fold a piece of A4 paper into three equal strips and rule a line across the centre. Draw a picture of yourself in the past at the top of one section and write about something you did in the past when you were younger. Now draw a picture of yourself as you are now, today. Write about yourself and what you are like at the moment. Finally, draw a picture of what you think you will look like in the future. Write about what you think you will be doing when you are a grown-up.

- Bring in some newspapers. Make explicit the connection between what is 'new', the 'news' and 'newspapers'. Ask the children to find the publication date on a newspaper.

- Compile a newspaper with the class sending out reporters to find out the latest facts from other classes or other members of staff.

- Produce a news programme with a group of children. Get each child in the group to write up their news. Construct a television out of a large cardboard box, cutting out the screen and drawing on the controls. Draw lots to see who will be the news reader. Present the programme to the rest of the class.

- Find out about other calendars and New Year traditions – Chinese, Hindu (Divali), Jewish (Rosh Hashanah), Muslim (Day of Hijrah) and Sikh (Baisakhi). These dates will have to be checked each year as most will vary. Enter them in the class diary.

The Chinese New Year

Discussion/Starting points

Find out the date when the Chinese New Year begins and which animal it is associated with. (There is a twelve year cycle, and each year is named after an animal.) Tell the children the story about how the years got their names (see story page 48).

Talk about the traditions associated with the Chinese New Year:
- cleaning the home during the last month of the old year
- paying off any money that is owed
- buying gifts for friends and relatives
- buying and putting up lucky papers (red scrolls with auspicious inscriptions written on them)
- 'seeing the old year out and the new year in' with the family
- visiting relatives and friends
- eating special food
- giving children red packets of 'lucky money'.

Vocabulary

'Kung hay fat Choi' – 'Wishing you to prosper', the traditional New Year greeting.

Collections

Chinese artefacts associated with the New Year – lucky papers, New Year cards, posters, mandarin oranges with green leaves, red packets for gifts of money, hanging decorations, model (not real!) firecrackers, miniature lions like those seen in the lion dance.

Look out for artefacts that show:

The deities
- the Kitchen God, the Door God and the God of Wealth

Symbolic objects
- peaches symbolising long life
- fish symbolising abundance
- pine or cypress trees which bear the wish for a vigorous old age
- well nourished children.

Pictures showing life in modern China (it is important to include contemporary pictures to avoid presenting an archaic and stereotyped image); other Chinese artefacts – Chinese bowls, chop sticks, Chinese cups, willow pattern plates, a wok; illustrated recipe books for cooking Chinese food; a variety of Chinese food products – tea, tinned bamboo shoots, tinned lychees, rice, noodles; samples of Chinese calligraphy, brushes and ink.

Use red, as a lucky colour, and gold, to symbolise the wish for prosperity, for an effective eye-catching display.

Activities

- Select one of the animals in the race and draw it in the centre of some white sugar paper. Use wax crayons but do not fill in any of the sky or the water. Use a 'wash' of diluted blue fluorescent paint for the background, then depict the water using wavy strips of blue and green Cellophane and strips of shiny blue and silver paper.
- Make simple masks and act out the story.
- Pretend that you are the ox. Write about how you nearly won the race and about how you feel. Was it fair that the rat won?
- Design and make your own money packets using red paper, then decorate with gold felt-tip pens.

The Chinese New Year

- Copy Chinese calligraphy to make lucky papers.
- Prepare three sets of cards – one set with each of the animals' names on; another set with 1st, 2nd, 3rd etc. written on; and a final set with ordinal numbers written as words. Ask the children to match up the three sets.
- Make a time line that starts in the year in which the children were born. Mark in the years with their 19-- numbers and their Chinese names.
- Obtain a menu from a local Chinese 'take-away' restaurant. Let each child select three preferred items but make it clear that it will be the three most popular dishes that will be purchased for the class to sample. Are there any children who are able to eat with chop sticks? Can others learn how to?

The Chinese New Year

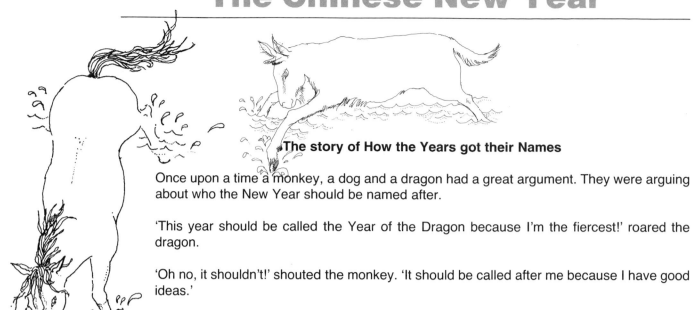

The story of How the Years got their Names

Once upon a time a monkey, a dog and a dragon had a great argument. They were arguing about who the New Year should be named after.

'This year should be called the Year of the Dragon because I'm the fiercest!' roared the dragon.

'Oh no, it shouldn't!' shouted the monkey. 'It should be called after me because I have good ideas.'

'What?' barked the dog. 'Why should it be named after you? It should be named after me. I work the hardest.'

'Oh no, you don't!' said the dragon and the monkey.

'Oh yes, I do!' said the dog.

And so they argued on, for hours and hours and hours. And as they argued, other animals came along to listen. But after a while they also joined in the argument. Each animal wanted the year named after itself.

'It should be the Year of the Tiger.'

'No it shouldn't. It should be the Year of the Horse.'

'But why? I'm the strongest. It should be the Year of the Ox.'

In the end there were twelve animals arguing together and soon a fight broke out. There was roaring and chattering, barking and growling, neighing and bellowing, squeaking and thumping, hissing and bleating, crowing and grunting. There was so much noise that it disturbed the gods in heaven.

'What on earth is the matter with those animals?' said one god to another. 'We'd better go and see what's happening.'

So the gods appeared in the sky. This gave all the animals such a fright that they stopped their arguing and stared up at the gods.

'Why are you making such a noise? What are you quarrelling about?' asked one of the gods.

All the animals started to answer at once. The noise was deafening.

The Chinese New Year

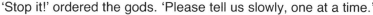

'Stop it!' ordered the gods. 'Please tell us slowly, one at a time.'

The animals bowed their heads. They were ashamed of their bad manners. One by one they explained the problem.

The gods thought it over and came up with an idea. They suggested that the animals held a race across a river. The New Year would be named after the winner of the race.

The animals liked the idea and each one thought that he would win. They rushed to the river bank and lined up ready for the start.

'On your marks! Get set! Go!' shouted the gods. And with a great splash all twelve animals jumped into the river and began swimming as fast they could towards the opposite bank.

The river was quite deep and there was a strong current, so it was ox, who was the strongest swimmer, who was soon in the lead. 'I'm going to win this race easily,' he thought. 'No problem.'

But he hadn't noticed rat who was swimming behind him. Rat was not a good swimmer, nor was he very strong, but he was very clever. He saw ox's tail just ahead of him, so he swam as hard as he could and managed to grab the end of the tail. He climbed up it without ox noticing, and tiptoed along ox's back.

Ox looked over his shoulder just to check he was still in the lead. He couldn't see rat who was sitting on his neck so ox felt sure that he was going to win. He was so pleased with himself that he laughed out loud. But as he did this he swallowed a big mouthful of water and began to cough and splutter.

Just at that moment rat jumped over the ox's head onto the river bank and squeaked 'I'm the winner!'

The gods agreed that rat was the winner. 'Hard luck, ox,' they said, 'You were the strongest but rat was too clever for you. This year will be the Year of the Rat and next year will be the Year of the Ox.'

One by one the other animals finished the race. Tiger was third, hare was fourth, dragon was fifth, snake was sixth, horse was seventh, goat was eighth, monkey was ninth, rooster was tenth, dog was eleventh and pig was twelfth, and last.

The gods congratulated all of the animals for finishing the race and decided to name a year after each animal in the order that they finished the race.

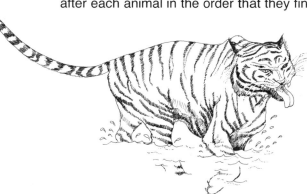

Ramadan and Eid-Ul-Fitr

Pre-arrangements

Find out when Ramadan (the Islamic month of fasting) begins. Start a collection of special books: old books, recently published books, favourite books, those with beautiful illustrations, pop-up books, other novelty books, family photograph albums, books about different faiths.

Discussion/Starting points

Which is your favourite book? Why is it special? Do you or your family have any special books at home?

Tell the children that Muslim families have a very special book called the Qur'an. Obtain a copy of this. As a mark of respect to the faith, wash your hands under running water immediately before handling the Qur'an. Make sure that the children also do this and that they treat the book with great care. After looking at the Qur'an do not leave it out on display but keep it carefully wrapped in a clean scarf on a high shelf above shoulder height.

Explain to the children that this time of year is a very special time for Muslim families. It is the time of Ramadan. Muslims believe that this was the time when God gave his message to the Prophet Muhammad. They believe that the Qur'an is special because it is God's message to everyone.

Vocabulary

Islam, Muslims (not Muhammadans as this is incorrect), Qur'an, Ramadan, Eid-ul-Fitr, 'Eid Mubarak' (the traditional Eid greeting), mosque, fasting, thinking, reflecting, praying, the poor, the needy, breaking fast, sunrise, sunset, lunar calendar, new moon, crescent moon, half moon, full moon, phases of the moon.

Collections

Pictures of mosques or Islamic artefacts; collections of artefacts – Qur'an stand, a prayer mat, subna (prayer beads), cards with Arabic script, vases or tiles with Islamic patterning. It would be most appropriate to display these artefacts against a green background.

Activities

Teachers should note that it is not appropriate to ask children to draw pictures of the Prophet Muhammad. There are no representations of him in any form of Islamic art work. Calligraphy, flowers, leaves and geometric patterns are traditionally used. It would also be unacceptable for the Prophet Muhammad to be portrayed dramatically.

- Tell the children the story about the Prophet Muhammad and the Old Woman (see page 51).
- Explain that all Muslims believe that they should help the poor. When it is Ramadan, Muslims fast because they are told to do so in the Qur'an. They pray to God and think about the poor. The grown-ups do not eat or drink anything between sunrise and sunset.
- Remind the children about the traditions associated with Lent. Talk about the origins of the word 'breakfast'. Bring in some dates for the children to sample. Explain that many Muslims break their fast each night by eating dates. Create a collage date palm using overlapping triangles for the trunk, and foil paper leaves.
- Explain how Ramadan begins when the new moon is first sighted. Talk about the lunar cycle. Read Eric Carle's book *I Want the Moon*, Hodder and Stoughton. Make a collage of the cycle using silver foil mounted on black paper. Write the labels with a silver pen.

Ramadan and Eid-ul-Fitr

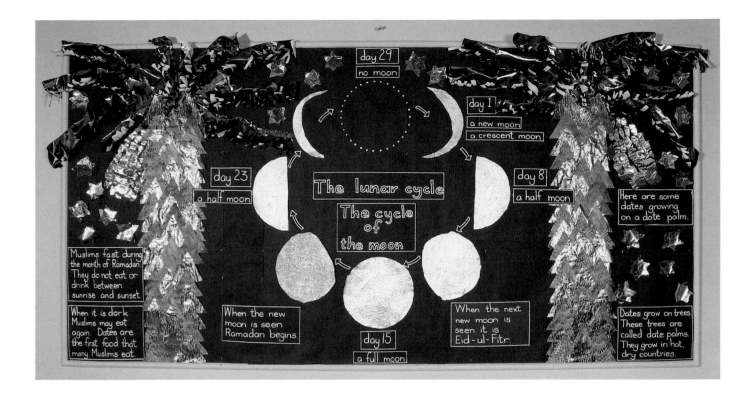

The following labels appear on the display:

day 29 / no moon

day 1 / a new moon / a crescent moon

day 23 / a half moon

The lunar cycle / The cycle of the moon

day 8 / a half moon

Here are some dates growing on a date palm.

Muslims fast during the month of Ramadan. They do not eat or drink between sunrise and sunset.

When it is dark Muslims may eat again. Dates are the first food that many Muslims eat.

When the new moon is seen Ramadan begins.

When the next new moon is seen it is Eid-ul-Fitr.

day 15 / a full moon

Dates grow on trees. These trees are called date palms. They grow in hot, dry countries.

The Prophet Muhammad and the Old Woman

The Prophet Muhammad was a very kind and a very wise man who lived nearly one thousand and five hundred years ago. But at the beginning not everyone liked him. This story is about one of those people.

Every day the Prophet Muhammad would go to a special building called a mosque to pray to God. On his way there he had to walk through the town and every day he went past the same houses. In one of these houses lived an old woman who did not like him. Every time he walked past she would brush the dust from her house over him, but every day the Prophet Muhammad would greet her saying 'Assalamu Alaikum' ('Peace be with you'). However, she would never answer him. She just kept on sweeping the dust over him.

But one day she was not there. There was no old woman and no dust. Now I think I would have rushed past thinking to myself 'Oh, I'm glad she's not there today.' But not the Prophet Muhammad. He went straight to her next-door neighbours to ask them where she was. They told him that she was very ill. So he went back to the old woman's house to look after her until she was better. He fetched her water, cooked her meals and cleaned her house. The old woman could not believe that it was the Prophet Muhammad who was helping her. She remembered how she had brushed dust over him and had never spoken to him. She felt sorry for what she had done and after that always tried to be a good Muslim.

Ramadan and Eid-ul-Fitr

- Explain how the month of fasting ends when the next new moon is seen. This is a very happy day and is called Eid-ul-Fitr. It is a day when:
  - new clothes are worn
  - Muslims go to the mosque
  - special food is cooked
  - Eid cards are exchanged
  - women put Mendhi patterns on their hands
  - Muslims give food or money to the poor.
- Talk about the different places that people go to when they pray – mosques, churches, chapels, cathedrals, gurdwaras, temples, synagogues.
- Tell the children the story of the mosque at Madina.

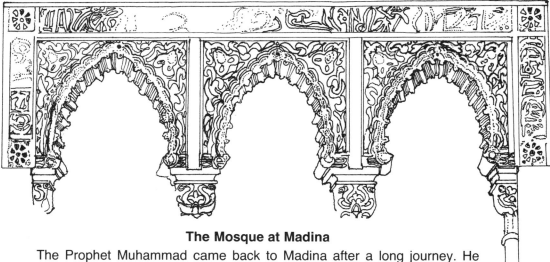

The Mosque at Madina

The Prophet Muhammad came back to Madina after a long journey. He came into the town riding his camel.

Everyone was really pleased to see him again. They rushed out of their houses to greet him and of course everybody wanted him to stay with them. The Prophet Muhammad said that he was going to build a mosque so that people could go there to pray to God. Everyone thought that this would be a good idea. Each person said that the mosque could be built on his land.

How was the Prophet Muhammad to choose? Everyone was being so kind and helpful. He did not want to upset anybody by not choosing them but he knew that he had to choose someone. What could he do?

He decided to let his camel choose. He let the reins go loose around the camel's neck. His camel walked along the dusty streets until it stopped next to a barn that was used for storing dates. Slowly the camel knelt on its front legs, then it lowered its back legs until it was sitting right down. It was on that very spot that the mosque was built.

There are many mosques all over the world. Many of them are very beautiful places where Muslim people can go to pray to God.

- Look at pictures of mosques. Make a model of a mosque using boxes and cylinders. Create the dome by using an aluminium foil basin sprayed with gold paint.
- Give the children tile-sized pieces of stiff card. Supply sticky paper in the traditional Turkish (Iznic) colours of royal blue, mid-blue, green and turquoise. Get the children to cut flower and leaf designs to glue on to their card tiles. Cover these with transparent self-adhesive film to give a 'glazed' effect (see display photograph).

- Make some Semian (a special sweet often eaten in Pakistan at Eid-ul-Fitr). You will need a knob of butter, 4oz vermicelli (broken in small pieces), 3 pints milk, sugar (about 6oz or to taste), a few ground cardamom seeds, chopped almonds and pistachios.

  Melt a large knob of butter in a heavy-based saucepan. Stir fry the vermicelli until golden brown (carefully, because this happens suddenly). Pour in milk and bring to boil, add ground cardamom seeds then lower heat and let milk simmer vigorously for about ½ hour. Add sugar and cook for further 5 mins. (should look like evaporated milk). Add nuts and pour in bowl. Can be served hot or cold.

- Make Eid cards. Remember that these will open from left to right. A picture of a mosque or the moon or a symmetrical geometric pattern would be suitable illustrations. Write the special Eid greeting of 'Eid Mubarak' inside the card. Try copying this message in Arabic.

- Obtain some henna powder from the hair products counter in a large chemist shop or department store. Mix up the henna powder with very hot water to make a thick paste. Take care not to get any of the henna mixture on to clothes as it will stain. Use a thin, stiff paintbrush to make henna paste patterns on the children's palms, having first obtained parental permission to do this. The children must leave their hands open flat for at least ten minutes before washing off the henna. The orange coloured hand pattern will last two or three days.
- Alternatively, get the children to draw round their hands, with their fingers spread out, using lead pencils on pastel sugar paper. Ask them to go over the outline with an orange wax crayon and then to draw patterns on the palms and fingers.

Pesach/Passover

Discussion/Starting points

Pesach (the Hebrew word for Passover) is a very special time for Jewish people. It is a family festival with everyone involved. It is a time for giving thanks and for remembering, a time for joy and happiness, and thinking about freedom. At Pesach the Jewish people celebrate the exodus of the Israelites from Egypt and their escape from slavery. The festival lasts for one week with special services on the first and last days. During the week only unleavened bread (Matzah) is eaten. This is because, in their haste, the Israelites did not have time to wait for the dough to rise, but simply baked flat loaves before they left. Pesach is also a Spring festival when houses must be cleaned – every crumb of leavened bread must be swept away. Some families will have special cutlery and dishes which have had no contact with risen flour or yeast. Jewish families celebrate Pesach with a special meal called a Seder. At the Seder, symbolic foods are eaten as the story of the exodus is told. The youngest member of each family has an important role to play, asking a series of special questions. As the questions are answered, the story of the escape from slavery unfolds.

Read the story of the exodus of the Israelites from Egypt.

Moses and the Exodus of the Israelites

The Israelites were very unhappy because the Pharaoh made them work so hard building for the Egyptians. They did not have their freedom and they were treated very unkindly. Their leader was called Moses. God sent Moses to the Pharaoh to say 'Let my people go!' but the Pharaoh kept saying 'No!'

God decided to help Moses and his people and he sent lots of plagues to try and make the Pharaoh change his mind and give in. God sent millions of frogs to jump all over the land. They were everywhere! The Pharaoh agreed that the Israelites could go, but when the frogs were gone he changed his mind and broke his promise, so God sent more plagues. He sent gnats, flies, boils and locusts. The cattle fell ill and died, and hail fell and ruined the crops in the fields. Each time the Pharaoh made false promises and pretended to give in, but when the plague stopped he changed his mind and refused to let the people go.

The last plague was that the oldest boy in each family should die. The houses of the Israelites were 'passed over' because they had marked their doors with a secret sign – the blood of a lamb. The Pharaoh was so upset that he immediately said that they could go. The Israelites wasted no time. They left as fast as they could. They didn't even wait for their bread to rise.

They travelled by day and by night, until they came to the Red Sea. Then suddenly they realised that the Pharaoh and his army were following them! Moses said to his people 'Do not be afraid. God will save us!'. God told them to carry on, and drove the sea back so that they could pass through the water walking on dry land. The Israelites could see a wall of water on both sides of them. They passed safely through, wondering at such an amazing sight. The Pharaoh's army followed close behind. As they reached the middle, God made the sea waters close over them and they were all drowned.

That is how God saved the Israelites and gave them their freedom. The people gave thanks to Moses and to God.

Talk about freedom. What does it mean to be free?

This is intended to be used as a focus for discussion, *not* as a tasting activity nor as a long-term display.

Activities

- Set a table for a Seder. Talk about the symbolism associated with each item.
  - A piece of lamb shankbone (not eaten) – this is connected with the use of lamb's blood to save the lives of the Israelites.
  - A roasted or baked egg dipped in salt water – representing the tears of the slaves, and also the Red Sea.
  - A spring vegetable or herb – sometimes parsley or lettuce – to signify new life and growth. This is also dipped in the salt water at the beginning of the ceremony.
  - A bitter herb – such as horseradish, or radish – to remind people of the harshness of slavery.
  - Haroset – a sweet paste that represents the mortar used by the slaves in building.

    Explain to the children that, as the story is told, Jewish families eat these foods, together with matzos and wine.
- Set up a separate tasting activity. Talk about contrasting tastes – sweet, sour, bitter, salty. Find out about different areas of the tongue where these tastes are sensed. Collect 'taste' vocabulary and display on a picture of a giant mouth with a giant tongue.
  - flavour, tang, savour, tastebuds, palate, seasoned, spicy, peppery, strong, tart, vinegary, sharp, salty, sweet, sour, bitter, watery, insipid, mild, delicious, yummy.
- Plant seeds to celebrate 'new life'. Observe and measure growth.
- Dramatise the story of Moses and the parting of the Red Sea.
- Find out about other Jewish festivals, e.g. Purim, Hannukah, and the special foods associated with them.
- Find out about the Torah, the scrolls, the ark. Visit a synagogue.
- Find out about the Jewish calendar, and the phases of the moon.
- Look at Hebrew print. Make a collection of books.

Easter

Discussion/Starting points

Easter is a very important festival for Christians. It is a time for remembering the death of Christ and for celebrating his resurrection. Easter customs are also linked to ancient celebrations of the end of winter and the coming of spring. The word Easter can be traced to Eostre, the goddess of spring, while Pâques (French), Pasqua (Italian) and Pascua (Spanish) come from the Jewish spring festival of Passover, or Pesach.

Before talking about the Easter story it is important to remind the children of the story of Jesus' birth and to tell stories about his life. This historical background is essential to show why Jesus was thought to be so special and why his enemies considered him to be such a threat to their power and authority. Read or tell the story of Jesus' triumphant entry into Jerusalem (Palm Sunday), the events of Good Friday and the crucifixion, and the mystery of the resurrection. A particularly sensitive and clear version is found in *Easter* by Gail Gibbons, Hodder and Stoughton.

Vocabulary

Lent, Mardi Gras, Passover, Eostre, simnel cake, fast, crucifixion, resurrection, Seder, Holy Week, Passion, the Last Supper, disciples, tomb, Christ, Messiah, Paschal candle.

Activities

- Make a class calendar that includes the whole period from the beginning of Lent to the end of Holy Week. Explain to the children that, unlike Christmas, Easter does not occur on the same date every year. This is because it is based on the phases of the moon. Easter takes place on the Sunday following the first full moon appearing on or after 21st of March – the Spring Equinox. During the forty day period of Lent, Christians prepare for Easter. Mark the special days on the calendar and talk about the main customs associated with each day.

SHROVE TUESDAY – the day before Lent. It is also called Mardi Gras in France. It is customary to eat up all the rich foods before Lent, so pancakes and oatcakes are made to use up the eggs.

ASH WEDNESDAY – the first day of Lent and marks the beginning of the fasting. Many Christians will give up something that they particularly like or enjoy.

MOTHERING SUNDAY – takes place on the fourth Sunday of Lent. Young people who worked away from home were traditionally allowed to visit their families before the Easter festival. They took home special presents to their mothers, e.g. some Spring flowers or a simnel cake.

PALM SUNDAY – on this day Christians remember how Jesus rode into Jerusalem on a donkey and how he was welcomed by the people waving branches of palm trees. Show the children a palm cross – the traditional symbol of Palm Sunday.

MAUNDY THURSDAY – the day on which Jesus shared a Last Supper with his disciples. Churches are cleaned and it is a custom to give money or gifts to the poor.

GOOD FRIDAY – Christians believe that Jesus was crucified on this day. It is a day of sadness and loss. People go to church and pray.

EASTER SUNDAY – the celebration of the resurrection, a time of hope and joy. Talk about the importance of Sundays to Christians – the day of the resurrection.

- Talk about the special foods associated with the Easter festival. Make a class recipe book.
- Talk about the idea of fasting. Find out about other religious festivals when it is customary to fast. Research the many customs associated with Pancake Day (Shrove Tuesday). On Good Friday 'hot cross buns' are eaten to remind us of the crucifixion. When Lent is over, Easter biscuits made with butter and spices are eaten, and chocolate Easter eggs are given. Eggs have long been regarded as a symbol of new life.

Easter

- Find out about other customs associated with Easter, e.g. egg-rolling, Easter bonnet parades and the wearing of new clothes, Easter egg hunts, the 'Easter Bunny' etc.
- Make Spring flower pictures. Look at colours associated with spring. Cut sponges into small triangles and leaf or petal shapes and print using pale colours on dark blue or purple paper.
- Egg pictures:
  - Cut out egg shapes from card. Decorate the shapes by gluing pasta and painting with fluorescent colours.
  - Cut out large egg shapes from white paper. Wet the paper and sprinkle with dry powder paint to create a speckled-egg effect.
  - Paint repeating patterns on giant egg-shapes and decorate with crêpe or Cellophane bows.
- Decorate hard-boiled eggs by dyeing them with cold-water dyes or 'natural' dyes by crayoning or drawing patterns with felt-tip pens, or by gluing on sequins and glitter. Make an Easter display of decorated eggs in baskets etc.
- Design and make an Easter garden.
- Collect stories about eggs.
- Write your own book of stories about eggs.
- Find out about different life-cycles.

Grain Harvest

Sowing by hand

Cutting wheat with a sickle

A corn store on stone mushroom legs to keep out rats

Windmill for grinding corn

Brick oven

Discussion/Starting points

At the very beginning of the Autumn Term ask the children these questions: Why have you just had such a long holiday? Why isn't the long holiday in November or February? Why is it always in August? Explain how in the past everyone, even the children, had to help harvest the wheat. What do we use wheat for? Who has been to a harvest festival in the church? What happened? Why was it a happy time? Help the children to understand that, in the past, the success or failure of the harvest could have been a matter of life or death. Talk about drought and famine in other parts of the world.

Vocabulary

Harvest, sickle, scythe, combine harvester, stubble, straw, bale, corn dolly, plait, thresh, winnow, chaff, husk, grain, bran, wheat germ, mill, miller, grindstones, flour, plain, self-raising, wholemeal, yeast, knead, prove, rise, bake, baker, loaf, crust, crumb, slice, toast, flat bread, oats, barley, rye, maize, millet, rice, short-grain, long-grain, risotto, paella, biryani, egg fried rice.

Collections

See photograph on opposite page.

Activities

Read the story of Little Red Hen. Discuss the stages by which wheat becomes bread. Make a flow chart to show the historical stages described in the story e.g. cutting with a sickle, storage in sacks, windmilling, baking in a coal or wood-fired stove. Now read *Thank you for a Loaf of Bread* by Patricia and Victor Smeltzer, a Lion Book. Discuss the stages involved in this story. Make a flow chart showing the modern stages, e.g. combine harvesting, storage in silos, shipping the grain, milling it in factories, baking in gas or electric fired ovens. Compare and contrast the two flow charts.

Seed drill

A combine harvester

Grain silos

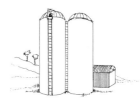

Flour mill

Modern oven

Grain Harvest

- Put some seeds in a polythene bag and crush them with a wooden mallet, or use a pestle and mortar, to make coarse flour.

- Make some leaven bread with yeast and some unleaven bread without yeast e.g. chappatis.

- What else is made from flour? Display illustrations in recipe books or collect pictures, packets or labels of other flour-based products e.g. rusks, croutons, biscuits, cookies, cakes, pastries, scones, buns, batter, Yorkshire pudding, pancakes, crêpes, semolina, bulghur, cous-cous, noodles, pasta.

- Weigh a cupful of pasta. Will it weigh more or less or exactly the same after cooking? Why? Cook the pasta and re-weigh. What has happened. Why?

- Visit a field, conservation area or roadside verge to look for wild grass seeds. Compare these seed heads with those of cultivated grains.

- Talk about the variety of grains grown in Britain and around the world. Get the children to bring in empty breakfast cereal boxes and read out the ingredients. Classify the products as being made from either wheat, maize, oats, rice or mixed grains (see photograph above).

- Ask each child to bring in an empty box of his/her favourite breakfast cereal. Make a bar chart using the boxes to show which is the most popular product.

- Fill a cup with popping corn. When this is cooked, how many cups of popcorn do you think it will make? Draw the corn before and after cooking. Measure how many cups of popcorn have been made.

- Make a drawing of a corn cob, carefully observing the colour and arrangement of the seeds.

- Weigh out ten grams of the following into polythene bags: wheat grains, white flour, wholemeal flour, rolled oats, oatmeal, popping corn, popcorn, cornflakes, rice grains, rice crispies. Hang the bags up and compare the relative volumes.

- Tell the children the Parable of the Sower (Matthew 13 1:9, Mark 4 1:9, Luke 8 4:8). Find stories about grain products for example, *The Magic Porridge Pot, The Runaway Pancake.*

Tropical Harvest

Discussion/Starting points

Before the children arrive, place a coconut in a 'Feely Box'. Put your hands in. Can you guess what it is. Don't tell us its name – keep it a secret! But please give us some clues! What does it feel like? What shape is it? What size is it? Is it light or heavy? Make a list of the descriptive words the children use.

Vocabulary

Tropical, hot, sunny, steamy, humid; fruits, pineapples, mangoes, paw-paws, papaya, bananas, melons, sugar cane; fresh, fruity, juicy, thirst-quenching, mouth-watering, sweet, delicious, ripe, succulent, creamy, fibrous, stone, seeds, skin, coconut, shell, milk, flesh, desiccated, palm tree; the West Indies, the Caribbean, Jamaica, Trinidad, Grenada, Malaysia, the Philippines, Sri Lanka, the Equator.

Collections

A coconut and coconut products – coconut cookies, coconut ice, desiccated coconut, tinned coconut milk, coir matting, coconut oil, soap or shampoo containing coconut oil; tins of cubed and sliced pineapple, an empty pineapple juice carton; tinned mangoes, mango chutney, an empty mango juice carton; a packet of dried banana chips. Pictures of tropical countries – selective pictures from holiday brochures can be used, although care needs to be taken to avoid stereotypical images.

Activities

- Make a drawing of the coconut, carefully observing the shape, the shades of colour and the coconut fibres.
- Make coconut palms (see illustration).

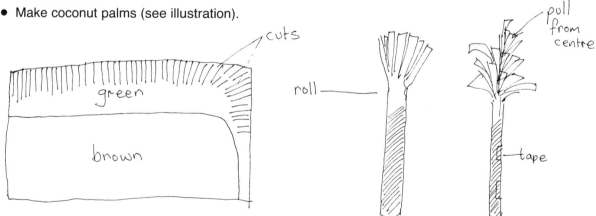

- Before weighing the coconut, estimate how many multi-link cubes you will need to balance against it. Weigh the coconut using a bucket balance. Was yours a good guess?
- Will the coconut float? Why do you think that? How can we find out? Before floating, make a note of what you think will happen – write 'yes' or 'no' on a slip of paper and stick it on to the prediction chart (teacher having pre-prepared chart). Was yours a good prediction? Why do you think it floated?
- The teacher can now make two holes in the top of the coconut. Use an awl or a hand drill to pierce the round marks at the top. Pour out the coconut milk for the children to sample. Make a bar graph to show who did and who did not like the taste.
- Now the teacher can saw the coconut in half carefully. Talk about the inside of the coconut. What did it look like? What did it smell like? What did it taste like? Make a list of the descriptive words that the children use. Using a brown felt-tip pen, write out these words and those generated earlier on to white circles of paper decorated with brown borders.

Tropical Harvest

- The children can make drawings of the inside of the two halves before sampling the flesh. Make a second bar graph to show likes and dislikes. Remember to save one half to hang out and attract blue tits and maybe other birds.

- Make coconut ice. Sample – and this time use beads threaded on to two strings to record how many children liked or disliked the sweet. (See illustration)

- Talk about other coconut products, including coir matting and coconut oil. Explain how the outer, hairy husk of the coconut is removed and used to make matting.

- Nearly all the activities described above can be successfully repeated substituting a watermelon for the coconut. The contrast in size, colour, weight, texture etc will generate a lot of discussion, as will its buoyancy. Why does something so big and heavy float?

- Use a wax resist technique for depicting the inside of the watermelon. Use dark green, white and brown wax crayons for the skin and seeds and then sponge print the flesh using dilute rose-coloured paint. Involve the children in accurate colour selection and mixing. Remind them that they must press hard with the crayons

Tropical Harvest

- Sample other fruits either singly or in a fruit salad. Use pineapple, bananas, mangoes, papaya, etc. Compare and contrast the colour, size, shape, smell, taste and texture of the fruit. Look at the seeds and stones. Are there many seeds or a single stone? Compare their colour, shape and size.
- Read 'Mango' by Grace Nichols, from *Come on into my Tropical Garden*, A & C Black.

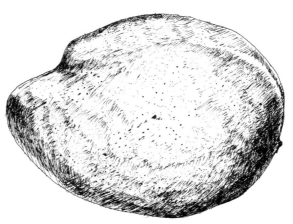

Mango

Have a mango
sweet rainwashed
sunripe mango
that the birds themselves
woulda pick
if only they had seen it
a rosy miracle
Here
take it from mih hand

Grace Nichols

- Look at the shape of a mango and compare it with a paisley pattern. Let the children design their own paisley patterns.
- Collect the labels from cans of tropical fruits and locate the countries of origin on a map. Display the labels round the edge of the map, make card flags to label each country and match label to flag with coloured thread.
- Copy these multi-lingual labels to use in classroom displays. Explain to the children that different languages may use different scripts.

pakwan
water melon
The Philippines
Tagalog

koko
coconut
The Seychelles
French Creole

荔 枝
lychee
China
Chinese

কলা
banana
Bangladesh
Bengali

buah nenas
pineapple
Malaysia
Bahasa Malay

- Talk about different tropical countries and find out if any of the children or members of their family have ever visited any of these countries. What can they remember about their visit? Have they any photographs?
- Read these stories set in the Caribbean:
  Emmanuel and his Parrot by Karl Craig, OUP.
  Emmanuel goes to Market by Karl Craig, OUP.

Divali

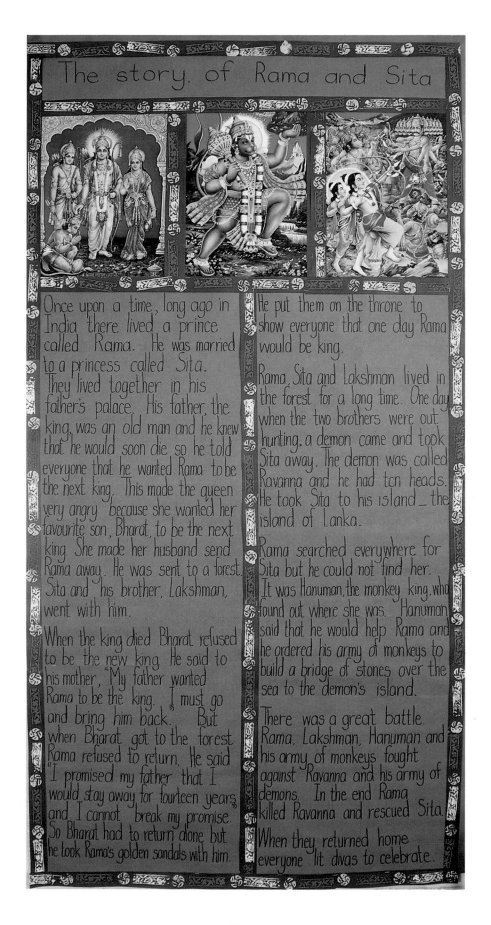

The story of Rama and Sita

Once upon a time, long ago in India there lived a prince called Rama. He was married to a princess called Sita. They lived together in his father's palace. His father, the king, was an old man and he knew that he would soon die so he told everyone that he wanted Rama to be the next king. This made the queen very angry because she wanted her favourite son, Bharat, to be the next king. She made her husband send Rama away. He was sent to a forest. Sita and his brother, Lakshman, went with him.

When the king died Bharat refused to be the new king. He said to his mother, "My father wanted Rama to be the king. I must go and bring him back." But when Bharat got to the forest Rama refused to return. He said "I promised my father that I would stay away for fourteen years and I cannot break my promise." So Bharat had to return alone but he took Rama's golden sandals with him.

He put them on the throne to show everyone that one day Rama would be king.

Rama, Sita and Lakshman lived in the forest for a long time. One day when the two brothers were out hunting, a demon came and took Sita away. The demon was called Ravanna and he had ten heads. He took Sita to his island – the island of Lanka.

Rama searched everywhere for Sita but he could not find her. It was Hanuman, the monkey king, who found out where she was. Hanuman said that he would help Rama and he ordered his army of monkeys to build a bridge of stones over the sea to the demon's island.

There was a great battle. Rama, Lakshman, Hanuman and his army of monkeys fought against Ravanna and his army of demons. In the end Rama killed Ravanna and rescued Sita.

When they returned home everyone lit divas to celebrate.

Divali

Discussion/Starting points

Read the story of 'Rama and Sita' (see photograph on previous page). Explain how their safe return was a reason for celebration. Talk about how everyone lit lamps (divas) to show that they were happy because Rama and Sita were safe. Explain that this story was first told a very long time ago in a country called India. Can you find India on this map/globe? Tell the children that the people in India still celebrate by lighting divas. Explain that this festival of lights is called Divali.

Talk about other traditions associated with Divali:

- worship in the home
- drawing Rangoli patterns using coloured rice flour or chalk on the ground at the entrances of homes (see photographs on page 65)
- wearing best clothes
- visiting family and friends
- eating delicious sweets
- watching fireworks.

Explain that Divali is celebrated in October or November. Its exact date is determined by the lunar calendar.

Teachers should note that there are many regional variations to the festival of Divali, e.g. the worship of Lakshmi, the goddess of wealth, by Gujarati Hindus, or the Sikh story that celebrates the release of Guru Har Gobind from prison (see page 66):

Rama and Sita is the most suitable story for dramatisation because it would not be appropriate for someone to enact the part of a Sikh Guru.

Vocabulary

Divali, divas, Rama, Sita, Hannuman, Ravanna, India, fireworks, light, celebrate, festival, special day, flame, shine, bright, sweets, share, visit, friends, relations.

Collections

Indian artefacts – divas, joss stick holders, dolls, small statuettes of Hindu deities, puppets, examples of Indian needlework, sari lengths etc; pictures showing Indian food, clothes etc; posters depicting Hindu deities; tinsel for highlighting the display. Look at the predominant colours in popular Indian posters when selecting backgrounds for display work.

Activities

- Paint pictures of characters from the story of Rama and Sita. Mix some PVA with the paint for greater adhesion so that once the pictures are dry, additional PVA can be applied, and glitter sprinkled on to the figures. Use strips of shiny coloured paper as a border for each picture.

- Make a firework display picture using a wax scrape or a wax resist technique.

- Buy or make some Indian sweets for the children to taste, e.g. barfi, halva, laddu, gulab jaman, rasgullas, jalebi.

- How to make barfi.
  You will need: 100 gm margarine, 150 gm sugar, 100 ml milk, 250 gm full cream milk powder, 60 gm ground almonds, a few ground cardamom seeds.
  Melt margarine in saucepan, add sugar and stir well. Add fresh milk and bring to the boil. Add cardamom seeds. Remove from heat and add powdered milk. Stir until smooth, mix in ground almonds. Grease a shallow tin, put mixture into tin and press down. Leave until cool and cut into squares .

- Make divas out of clay or other quick-drying modelling material (see illustration). Place a night light in each diva. Traditionally oil and wicks are used, but this would be unsafe in schools.

Divali

- Make a 'mirror work' Divali card to send to family or friends to wish them 'a happy Divali'.

Make 'mirror work' Divali cards. Fold a square of thin card and cut out semi-circles from along the crease.

Now re-fold the card,   fold the card diagonally   and diagonally again.

Using felt-tip pens, make coloured designs around each of the circular holes, then fill in the background in a single colour. Glue the card on to an identically sized piece of silver foil and mount the whole thing on to a piece of coloured card. Add a border of silver using a silver felt-tip pen.

- If possible, obtain some wooden Indian printing blocks to use with fluorescent paints on black sugar paper. Otherwise create similar patterns by carving shapes into potato halves for the children to use.

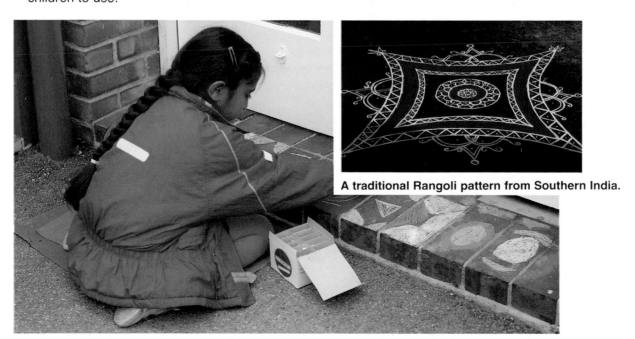

A traditional Rangoli pattern from Southern India.

Children will enjoy designing their own Rangoli patterns.

Divali

- Use coloured chalks to decorate a step with Rangoli patterns.
- Make a Divali card with a diva on.

Cut out a diva and its flame in shiny foil and glue on to a square of black sugar paper. Now draw a chalk line around the flame. Create a 'radiating light' effect by brushing the chalk outwards using a dry paint brush. Repeat this process with additional chalk lines. Fixative may be sprayed on the chalk by the teacher in a well-ventilated room. The diva picture can then be mounted on to a folded card.

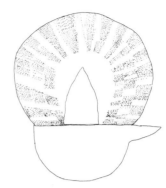

- Tell the story of Guru Har Gobind's release from prison.

Sikhs have a special reason for celebrating Divali. Coloured lights are lit in the Gurdwaras (Sikh temples) and children are given presents. Sikhs remember that it was at Divali, many years ago, that Guru Har Gobind was let out of prison. This is how it happened.

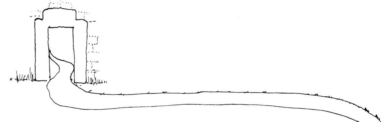

Guru Har Gobind

Guru Har Gobind had been sent to prison by some of Emperor Jahangir's men. He had been in prison some time and he had become friends with the other prisoners. But these were no ordinary prisoners – they were 52 Indian princes! The Emperor Jahangir decided to find out for himself why Guru Har Gobind was in prison so he sent for the Guru. But Guru Har Gobind would not leave the prison! He said that he would only go if his 52 friends could go with him!

Well, the Emperor did not want so many prisoners to leave the jail all at the same time, so he sent this message to Guru Har Gobind, 'You may leave the prison and the princes may go with you . . . but, they must be holding on to the clothes that you are wearing, and as you go you must leave through the narrow prison gateway.' What were the princes and Guru Har Gobind to do? The gateway was so narrow that maybe only two or three would be able to get through and still touch the Guru's clothes. But Guru Har Gobind had a clever idea! He ordered a special cloak to be brought to him. It was very long and it had 52 silk tassles sewn on to it. He put on the cloak and left through the narrow gateway. His 52 friends followed, each one holding on to a silk tassel.

Advent – the Spiders' Christmas

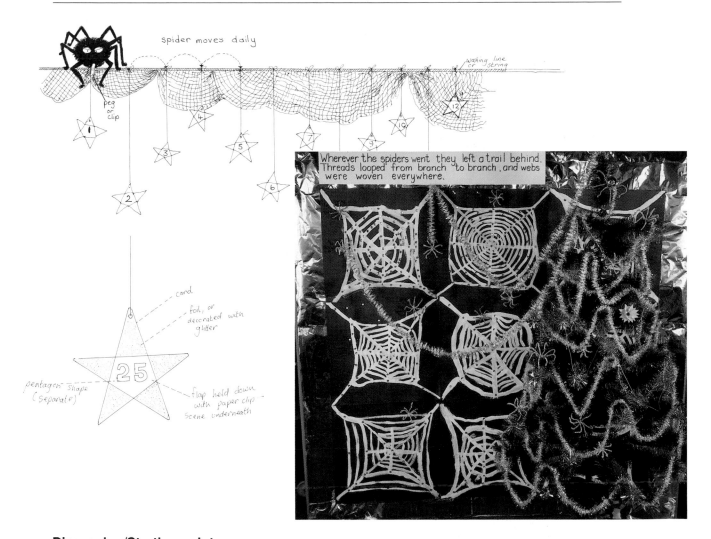

spider moves daily

washing line or string

peg or clip

card

foil, or decorated with glitter

25

pentagon shape (separate)

flap held down with paper clip Scene underneath

Wherever the spiders went they left a trail behind. Threads looped from branch to branch, and webs were woven everywhere.

Discussion/Starting points

Read the story of Christkindel and the Christmas spiders. Talk about preparations for Christmas – choosing a Christmas tree, decorating it, making Christmas decorations and presents for your friends, cleaning the house, and inviting friends to visit. The period before Christmas is called Advent. What do you do in your house to prepare for Christmas? Talk about the sharing of Christmas, the giving and receiving of gifts. How do you feel on Christmas Eve?

Talk about the anticipation, the excitement of waiting. How many days are there in December? Look at a calendar and find Christmas Day and Boxing Day. On 1st December, start opening the windows of an Advent calendar to count down the days until Christmas. For Christians, Advent is a period of hope and quiet expectation. Talk about Advent customs such as the lighting of candles on an Advent crown.

Activities

- Make Advent calendars:
  - A giant web. Glue the windows around the web in a spiral pattern with the final window in the centre.
  - Stars on a string (as shown in the sketch).
  - Make an Advent crown with four candles and evergreen foliage. One candle is lit each week in the four weeks leading up to Christmas. A fifth candle is added in the middle.
- Dramatise the story. Characters – spiders, village children, barn animals, pets etc. The spiders can decorate the tree with tinsel, then fairy lights can be switched on when Christkindel works the 'magic'.

Advent – the Spiders' Christmas

- Decorate a Christmas tree with tinsel – gold and silver threads to represent the spiders' cobwebs. Make dough shapes to hang on the tree. Cut out stars and crescents. Slow bake to harden them, then varnish or paint them with PVA glue. Hang them on the tree with silver or gold thread.
- Spiders' web paintings. Paint web shapes with white, silver or gold powder paints on black paper. Glue sequins or glitter at the intersections of the web. Make a spider with pipe cleaners (silver and gold if possible) and position it on the web.
- Make presents for your family and friends. Bake cookies and gingerbread like Tante did and put them in decorated boxes tied with ribbons.

The Spiders' Christmas

It was time to get ready for Christmas. Tante cleaned her house, taking great care to sweep all the spiders' webs and cobwebs out from all the corners of her cottage. She went out into the woods to look for a Christmas tree. She chose a beautiful tall and straight tree, and took it back to her house to decorate. Next, Tante made lots of cookies to hang on the tree. Then she made special presents for her friends, for her pets and for all the animals in the barn. Everyone was remembered except for the spiders, for they had been swept away. Tante invited the animals and all the village children into her cottage to celebrate Christmas Eve. The children were excited and were wondering what presents Christkindel would bring them. They all came to see Tante's tree – it was so beautiful! As Tante fell asleep that night she made a special Christmas wish that something magical might happen. When she was asleep all the spiders gathered outside her door. They wanted to be part of Christmas too. They wanted to see the tree and all of the presents. As Christkindel passed by they asked if he would open the door for them. He let the spiders in!

Huge spiders, tiny spiders, smooth spiders, hairy spiders, spotted
spiders, brown and black and yellow spiders, and the palest kind
of see-through spiders came
creeping, crawling, sneaking softly, scurrying,
hurrying, quickly, lightly, zigging, zagging,
weaving, and wobbling into the old woman's cottage.
The curious spiders crept closer and closer to the tree

and, before Christkindel could stop them they had scampered from branch to branch, leaving a trail of cobwebs behind them. Christkindel was horrified – what would Tante say? She had worked so hard to clean her cottage ready for Christmas. So, Christkindel turned the spiders' webs into silver and gold threads of sparking tinsel. When Tante woke up she was amazed! Her Christmas wish had been granted. From that time onwards Tante always left the webs in the corners of her cottage so that the spiders could share her Christmas. On her tree she hung silver and gold tinsel to remind her of that magical Christmas Eve.

Story based on, and extract from, *The Cobweb Christmas*, by Shirley Climo, Hamish Hamilton. Another version is *The Little Christ Child and the Spiders* by Jan Peters, MacDonald.

Baboushka

Discussion/Starting points

Read or tell the story of Baboushka Find Russia on a map or globe. Talk about how big the country is. Tell the children that Baboushka means grandmother in Russian. Talk about the story. What was Baboushka like? Where do you think that the three kings were going? Why were they following a star? Who do you think they were going to see? Do you think that Baboushka should have gone with them immediately, or was she right to finish her work? How did she feel when she found out that she was too late? Have you ever felt disappointed? Read or tell the Christmas story. Remind the children of the gifts the wise men had brought for Jesus (Matthew 2). When do we give presents to other people? Why do we give presents?

Activities

- Find out how to write 'grandmother' in other languages. Match the different versions on to a world map to display.
- Find out about present bringers in other countries, e.g. Santa Claus, Father Christmas, St. Nicholas, Grandfather Frost, Befana.
- Read Babette Cole's *Beastly Birthday Book, Heinemann.* Make your own book of presents. Glue envelopes on to the pages and put pictures of presents inside.
- Look at Russian writing. Display the Russian alphabet alongside the English alphabet. Compare and contrast them.
- Paint large Russian dolls as shown in the photograph. Use the colours of Russian dolls – red, purple, yellow and green. Display with silver and gold stars.
- Find other stories about searching – journeys and quests.
- Tell the Christmas story from Baboushka's point of view.
- Tell Baboushka's story from the three kings' point of view.
- Write a play script and dramatise the story of Baboushka. Baboushka's journey could take her all over the world, discovering Christmas customs.

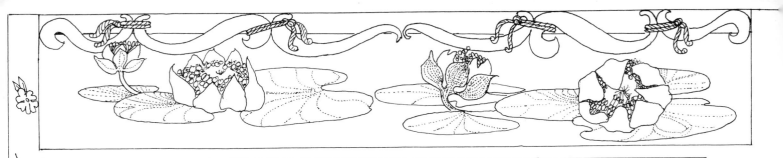

The story of Baboushka

One day Baboushka was as busy as ever, washing, cleaning, cooking and polishing, when she heard lots of talking outside. 'I wonder what's happening?' she said. When she went outside she could hardly believe her eyes! She saw three magnificent kings dressed in splendid clothes. They were obviously very tired and travel-weary and they were looking about them for somewhere to stay. 'This looks like a fine house,' they said, 'May we stay here?' Then Baboushka suddenly realised they were talking about her house. 'Come on in', she said, 'you look as if you've been up all night'. 'We have!' said the kings. While they were eating the delicious breakfast that Baboushka had prepared, the three kings introduced themselves and explained why they were travelling far from home. Balthasar, Caspar and Melchior told Baboushka about their search to find a new baby king. 'We were told to look for a new star in the sky and to follow it until we found him. We're taking him some presents of gold, frankincense and myrrh.'

'I was wondering what was in those interesting parcels,' said Baboushka, 'but aren't they funny presents for a baby? If I was going I would give him toys.' 'Why don't you come with us then?' asked the kings. 'I might if I'm ready in time', said Baboushka.

Well, all day long Baboushka worked hard as the three kings slept. She collected together lots of toys and presents that she thought the new baby would like. Night fell and the three kings got ready to leave. 'Will you be coming with us, Baboushka?' they asked. 'I'm not quite ready yet,' she replied. 'You go on ahead and I'll catch you up when I've finished cleaning the house.'

The three kings set off as soon as the star appeared in the night sky. They were so excited.

'Don't be too long, Baboushka,' they called.

The old lady worked all through the night, polishing and cleaning. 'The baby is going to love these presents,' she thought. Before she knew it, the sun had risen and was shining brightly. Baboushka was so tired that she was soon fast asleep and dreaming of her exciting journey. When Baboushka woke up she ran to her window to look for the star. 'Oh, no! The star has disappeared. Maybe if I hurry I'll catch them up,' she said, and picking up all her parcels, she rushed after the three kings. She asked at every village and at every town as she went, 'Have you seen a bright star in the sky? Have you seen three kings pass by? Do you know where I can find the new baby king?' But it was no use, no one could help her.

Some people say that Baboushka is still searching for the baby king. Every year she travels from house to house, hoping to find him there, and leaving presents just in case . . .

Book references

Brothers and Sisters, Sue Perry and Norma Wildman, Celebrations series, A & C Black.

Dat's New Year, Linda Smith, Celebrations series, A & C Black.

Faiths and Festivals, Martin Palmer, Ward Lock Educational.

Festivals, Jean Gilbert, OUP.

Festive Occasions, Judy Ridgeway, OUP.

Food, Ed. Rachel Gregory, in Exploring a Theme series, Christian Education Movement.

Gifts and Gift Bringers, Ed. Judith Lowndes, in Exploring a Theme series, Christian Education Movement.

Introduction to Popular Traditions and Customs of Chinese New Year, Chinese Community Centre (London Chinatown) and Guanghwa Co. Ltd., London.

Marvellous Stories from the Life of Muhammad, M.A. Tarantino, The Islamic Foundation.

The Oxford Book of Food Plants, G.B. Masefield et al, OUP.

Religion in the Multi-Faith School, Ed. by W. Owen Cole, Hulton Educational.

Religious Education Topics for the Primary School, John Rankin, Alan Brown and Mary Hayward, Longman.

Sam's Passover, Lynne Hannigan, Celebrations series, A & C Black.

The Sikhs, Their Religious Beliefs and Practices, W. Owen Cole and Piara Singh Sambhi, Routledge and Kegan Paul.

Spring Festivals, Mike Rosen, Wayland.

Spring Term, Dorothy J. Taylor, B.F.S.S. National R.E. Centre.

Stories in the Multilingual Classroom, ILEA Learning Resources.

Weather, Tony Potter, BBC Books.

for details of further Belair publications
please write to:
Belair Publications Ltd.,
P.O. Box 12,
Twickenham,
TW1 2QL,
England.

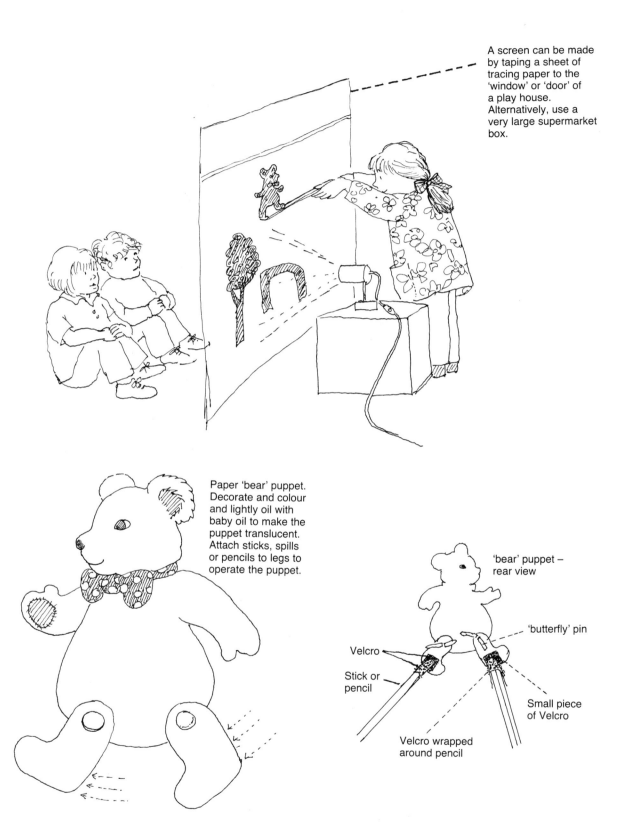

A screen can be made by taping a sheet of tracing paper to the 'window' or 'door' of a play house. Alternatively, use a very large supermarket box.

Paper 'bear' puppet. Decorate and colour and lightly oil with baby oil to make the puppet translucent. Attach sticks, spills or pencils to legs to operate the puppet.

'bear' puppet – rear view

'butterfly' pin

Velcro

Stick or pencil

Small piece of Velcro

Velcro wrapped around pencil